teach®
yourself

C++

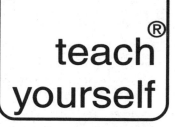

teach®
yourself

C++
second edition

richard riley

For over 60 years, more than 40
million people have learnt over
750 subjects the **teach yourself**
way, with impressive results.

be where you want to be
with **teach yourself**

For UK orders: please contact Bookpoint Ltd., 130 Milton Park, Abingdon, Oxon OX14 4SB. Telephone: +44 (0)1235 827720. Fax: +44 (0)1235 400454. Lines are open 09.00–18.00, Monday to Saturday, with a 24-hour message answering service. You can also order through our website www.madaboutbooks.com

For USA order enquiries: please contact McGraw-Hill Customer Services, PO Box 545, Blacklick, OH 43004-0545, USA. Telephone: 1-800-722-4726. Fax: 1-614-755-5645.

For Canada order enquiries: please contact McGraw-Hill Ryerson Ltd., 300 Water St, Whitby, Ontario L1N 9B6, Canada. Telephone: 905 430 5000. Fax: 905 430 5020.

Long renowned as the authoritative source for self-guided learning – with more than 30 million copies sold worldwide – the *Teach Yourself* series includes over 300 titles in the fields of languages, crafts, hobbies, business, computing and education.

British Library Cataloguing in Publication Data
A catalogue record for this title is available from The British Library.

Library of Congress Catalog Card Number: On file.

First published in UK 2003 by Hodder Headline Plc., 338 Euston Road, London, NW1 3BH.

First published in US 2003 by Contemporary Books, A Division of The McGraw-Hill Companies, 1 Prudential Plaza, 130 East Randolph Street, Chicago, Illinois 60601 USA.

The 'Teach Yourself' name is a registered trade mark of Hodder & Stoughton Ltd.

Copyright © 1999, 2003 Richard Riley

Typeset by MacDesign, Southampton
Printed in Great Britain for Hodder & Stoughton Educational, a division of Hodder Headline Plc, 338 Euston Road, London NW1 3BH by Cox & Wyman Ltd., Reading, Berkshire.

Impression number   10 9 8 7 6 5 4 3 2

Year   2007 2006 2005 2004 2003

contents

preface

C++ is a powerful language, but its structure is consistent and transparent, making it ideal even for complete beginners. This book assumes no previous programming experience, and introduces concepts and techniques that apply not only to C++ and its predecessor C, but to many other modern languages such as Java.

You won't be bombarded with the technicalities of low-level hardware, but you will be given a good enough idea of what is *really* happening to let you write fast, efficient and effective programs. All you need to get started is a computer and a good understanding of its basic functionality.

The examples in *Teach Yourself C++* are all text-mode programs, which means they will work with MS-DOS, the Microsoft Windows command prompt, MacOS, Linux, and many other modern operating systems.

The code samples in this book are purely illustrative and do not include the error-checking capability that is a key part of real-world program code. Although you are free to use them however you wish, neither the author nor the publisher may be held liable for any loss, damage or similar misfortune they might cause. That said, it is highly unlikely that your programming errors will result in anything worse than a temporary system hang.

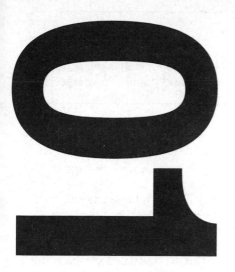

01

introducing C++

In this chapter you will learn

- the history of C++
- what a compiler is
- how to build your first program

Aims of this chapter

This chapter introduces C++ and the tools that you need for programming in this versatile and popular language.

1.1 What is C++?

C++ is a development of the C programming language originated in the early 1970s at AT&T labs. Like its predecessor, C++ combines the ease-of-use of a high level language with the functionality and capability of assembler, making it the language of choice for hundreds of different platforms and implementations. C++ is a *compiled* language, which means that the code written by the programmer must first be translated into machine instructions before it can be run. This job is performed by a special software package known as a *compiler*, which is used to create a program file that will run on the host computer. C++ code is easily portable as C++ compilers are available for many different platforms, so a program written for a DOS machine can be re-compiled and executed on a UNIX machine without too much difficulty.

1.2 Why use a compiler?

A compiler lets you write programs in a human-readable, easily maintained and understood format, instead of having to write out the numerically-encoded instructions that the computer understands. The exact syntax of the human-readable format depends on the language you have chosen to use; we will be using C++, but we could also try C, Pascal, Perl, BASIC, Java, COBOL, Fortran, Ada, or any of the numerous variants thereof. All of these have their uses and advantages, but you are going to learn C++ because it is widely used and very powerful.

Whatever the language, the compiler has the same basic functions, although different languages place more or less emphasis on each. Consider this line of code:

```
if (LoopCount > 10) CheckFileNames();
```

You do not even need to understand C++ to guess that if the value of 'LoopCount' (whatever that is) becomes greater than 10, the program does something called 'CheckFileNames'. In this one line, several of the most important features of the compiler are demonstrated.

- The compiler does a great deal of work for you. When it comes across a line, it writes out all the necessary machine instructions to achieve the result that you want.

- The compiler lets you use symbolic names. When the processor jumps to a new piece of code, it goes to a numeric address in the memory. Similarly, when it tries to get data from some area of storage, it takes the bytes starting from some numeric address in memory. Keeping track of all these addresses would be extremely difficult, especially as they are likely to change as the program is developed. What the compiler does is let you assign proper names to chunks of memory, so instead of trying to operate on 'the value at address d300:02f6' you operate on 'LoopCount' – a far more meaningful way of working.

- The compiler performs a lot of *type checking*. When you assign a name to a certain chunk of memory you also tell the compiler exactly how big that chunk is and what kind of information it is supposed to represent – in other words, you give that piece of data a type. This allows the compiler to check your code and catch a lot of errors before you run the program and find that everything crashes horribly. For example, if you had specified that 'LoopCount' was supposed to store a string of letters, the compiler would tell you that you had made a mistake when you tried to say 'if (LoopCount >10)'. Obviously, there is no way of comparing a string of letters with the number 10, but if you had been writing in raw machine code, this error would only have arisen when you tried to run the program, and would have been difficult to trace.

- Programs that are compiled are much easier to maintain. Most compiled languages allow code to be broken into chunks called functions. Functions can be passed information (*arguments*) when they are invoked (*called*), and they can return information back to the previous part of the program (the *caller*) when they are finished. This structuring facility allows more efficient coding and also encourages modularity – you could use the same function or set of functions (a *module*) in several different programs. In the example above, 'CheckFileNames()' is a function. This imaginary function does not take any arguments, but if it did, they would be placed between the (parentheses).

- By using a compiler, you can make your code *portable*. Because the source code is only converted to machine instructions by the compiler, the same program can be made to run on different systems (e.g. IBM PC or Macintosh) by changing the compiler. There are C or C++ compilers available for hundreds of different platforms.

1.3 The code linker

Almost every compiler has a companion, called a *linker*. The compiler does the bulk of the work by translating all the human-readable words, but it does not output a ready-to-run program. Instead, you get a file full of *object code*. This code contains machine-level instructions, but the symbolic names mentioned earlier are still in there. Then, the linker takes over, converting the object code into something that the operating system (e.g. MS-DOS) will actually recognize as a program. Why do it in this two-stage way? The reason is that the linker is capable of linking *several* object files together. Depending on the number of other files being thrown in, the numerical addresses of all those symbolic names will be different, so it is up to the linker, and not the compiler, to finalize them all into absolute values before the final '.com' or '.exe' file is produced.

The beauty of this system is that it allows programmers to create modular software – reusing components over and over again. Suppose you had written a set of functions to make conversions back and forth between several obscure units of measurement. Now, you want to make use of them in a new program. There are two ways of achieving this:

- You copy all the original code for your conversion functions and paste it straight into the source code for your new program. This works fine, but it means that every time you want to compile your new program to test it, the compiler has to work its way through all the code for the conversions as well. If these are reasonably hefty functions, this could take time, and is pointless as you are not making any changes to that part of the code.

- You compile the functions into a separate object file. Then, when you come to write your new program, you tell the linker to add in these functions before building the final program. This way, you never have to compile the functions again, and they are stored in a convenient package out of the way of your main project until they are needed. You could even distribute the object file for the conversions to other programmers – they can make full use of the functions without ever being able to see your own top secret source code that created them.

To improve the organization and structure of a project, multiple object files are sometimes built into a *library* file. The linker searches the library file for the code that it needs and links whichever embedded object files are required by the program.

The mechanism of code libraries is particularly applicable to C and C++, and is what makes these languages so popular with serious developers. The reason all software for Microsoft Windows looks the same is that all the functions for displaying windows, buttons and menus are in fact part of a standard set of libraries – so you can see that this system extends even to the most advanced levels.

Originally, the compiler and the linker were supplied as separate programs that were run from the command prompt. You would write your code in a text editor, save it, quit back to the prompt, then run the compiler and the linker in turn. This process was greatly simplified with the introduction of the Integrated Development Environment (IDE) which allows source editing, compiling, linking, debugging and project management all within a single software 'shell'. Almost all compilers available today work on this principle, and some incorporate many more advanced features to aid rapid development of applications.

1.4 Getting started

Before you can start learning C++, you need to get hold of some compiler software. You don't need the latest version (the previous releases are often sold off at very competitive prices) but before you go any further you do need to make sure that you have the software correctly installed on your computer and that as far as you can make out it runs without problems. DOS or Windows users can download DJGPP, an excellent free C++ development suite, from http://www.delorie.com/djgpp/. Most Unix and Linux distributions support C++ as part of the GNU Compiler Collection, which is available from http://www.gnu.org/software/gcc/. If you have to install GCC yourself, I recommend using the pre-compiled binaries.

Once you have a working installation, you are ready to run your first program! It has become something of a tradition that whenever programmers start learning to use a new language or application programming interface, the first thing they do is write a program to display the words 'Hello, World!' on the screen. This is actually more a test that the compiler is working correctly than of the programmer's ability, but it serves as an excellent starting point for our course.

Here is the code listing in full. Be sure to type it as shown, as even the smallest omission may prevent the program from compiling properly. The words and other characters must be exact for the code to compile; the layout is just to make it more readable. You can use either multiple spaces or a tab to indent the two middle lines – laying them out in this way makes it easier to visualize blocks of code. As you will see in later examples, there will often be two or more levels of indenting, as blocks are nested within blocks.

```
/* hello.cpp - A First Test Program
Author: Richard, 28/11/99 */

#include <iostream.h>

int main()
{
    cout << "Hello, World!\n";
    return 0;
}
```

Building and running your first program can be a struggle, so here are some instructions for a number of common compilers. If all else fails, try reading the documentation that came with your software!

- For DJGPP, open a DOS command prompt and type 'rhide' to start the development environment. Select **New** from the **File** menu and type in the code shown above, then choose **Save As** from the **File** menu and save the code as *hello.cpp* in the default directory. Select **Run** from the **Compile** menu and DJGPP will build *hello.exe* and run it. You can view the output by choosing **User Screen** from the **Windows** menu.

- For Borland Turbo C++, simply type 'tcc' to start the development environment and then follow the instructions given for DJGPP.

- For Microsoft Visual C++, launch the program from the Windows start menu. Select **New** from the **File** menu and choose **Win32 Console Application** from the list of standard projects available. Continue through the dialog boxes, selecting **Empty Project** when prompted. Select **New** from the **File** menu and this time choose **C++ Source Files** from the list. Make sure that the **Add to Project** checkbox is enabled. Type the code into the text window, select **Save** from the **File** menu, then **Build hello.exe** from the **Build** menu. If the program compiles without errors, run it by choosing **Execute hello.exe** from the **Build** menu.

- For GCC on Unix, use your favourite text editor to create a file containing the source code as shown above, and save it as *hello.cpp*. Return to the shell prompt (or start a second xterm) and type 'gcc -c hello.cpp -o hello' to compile the program. Run the program by typing './hello' at the prompt.

If you are successful, the program should print the message "Hello, World!" when it is run. Remember that you may need to choose **output window** to switch viewing between the IDE and the program's output. If you quit back to the command prompt, you should see a new file *hello.exe* which is the program you have just created. This file is completely independent of all the source files used to create it – once built, it can be run on any compatible computer.

Code on-line

The code samples in this book can all be downloaded from my Web site at **http://tyc.oxtale.com**

1.5 Understanding the code

It's time to get started looking at the various features of a C++ program, as illustrated in the **hello.cpp** example that you saw above. Breaking the code down into small, functional chunks is the easiest way to analyse its behaviour:

```
/* hello.cpp - A First Test Program

Author: Richard, 28/11/99 */
```

The first two lines in the file are probably the simplest to understand. What you see here is a *comment* – a piece of text that is completely ignored by the compiler. Comments are used to explain to a reader what the code is doing at any point, and should be used liberally – it is all too easy to come back to a large program after a few months and find that you have completely forgotten the thought processes that went into it! Here, the comment is started with /* and ended with */ – anything between these two markers is disregarded.

Single line comments are useful for short notes. They start with two forward slashes like this // and stop at the end of the line, for example:

```
if (LoopCount>10) GetFileNames(); // comments go here
```

Or alternatively:

```
// comments could go here too
if (LoopCount>10) GetFileNames();
```

Next, we have an example of what is called a preprocessor directive, identified by the hash character # at the beginning of the line.

```
#include <iostream.h>
```

This is actually an instruction to the compiler to copy the entire contents of the file **iostream.h**, which comes as part of every

C++ compiler package, into your source code at the current point. This happens before the code is run through the main translation process, and is necessary because **iostream.h** contains a number of important definitions needed by the compiler before the program will work. The mechanism is explained in a later chapter; all you need know at the moment is that this line must be added at the beginning of your code in order for certain things to compile correctly.

At last, we come to the code itself:

```
int main()
{
    cout << "Hello, World!\n";
    return 0;
}
```

What you see here is the implementation of a small function (i.e. a block of code that performs a certain task) called **main**. The first line gives the name of the function, and the word **int** means that the function will return an integer value when it has completed. The name **main** is special because it marks the point where the program starts running, so whenever the operating system loads the program into memory, it passes control to this function first. Since every program needs a place to start, the compiler will always look for this function and will report an error if it can't find it.

Notice that the body of the function is enclosed by {curly braces}. These characters are often used in C++ syntax to mark the start and end of a functional group of statements. By laying these out one above the other, it is much simpler to see where the blocks start and end – and to check that you have the opening and closing braces for each block.

Here, there are just two statements (one on each line) but a C++ statement can spread over as many lines as you wish. Statements are made up of any valid combination of words and symbols, and are ended with a semicolon.

```
cout << "Hello, World!\n";
```

The first statement is made slightly unusual by the use of the angle brackets << to separate the word **cout** and the phrase **"Hello, World!\n"** – this, unfortunately, is not conventional C++ syntax (it relies on an advanced technique, *operator over-*

load, covered in Chapter 10) but for now it is enough to know that by using **cout << [*data*]** you can output any kind of data to the screen. Here, we are using it to print the words "Hello, World!", but the same syntax is used to display any kind of numeric data.

    return 0;

The second of the two statements is much simpler. Since the function we are in was declared **int main()**, the last thing the function must do before ending is return an integer – here, we return zero. This return value is normally sent back to whichever part of the program called the function in the first place. However, since it is the operating system itself that calls **main**, the return value can be used to signal whether or not the program completed successfully.

Summary

In this chapter you were introduced to C++, a portable and very widely used compiled language. We covered the reasons for using a compiler, including the ability to use symbolic names, perform data type checking and to write efficient, modular code. You have also been introduced to the linker, which allows several object and library files to be built into a single program file, and the concept of an IDE (Integrated Development Environment) which automates many of the processes involved in editing, compiling and linking code.

We broke down a very simple C++ program to analyse the various elements, and discussed comments, functions and statements. In particular, you learnt about the significance of the **main** function, and you already know how to output words and phrases to the screen.

You are also about to discover that learning to program is made much easier by trying out concepts as you read them. At the end of this and every chapter, is a selection of exercises for you to test your new-found knowledge.

Exercises

1 Get hold of a C++ compiler package and install it on your computer.

2 Type the "Hello, World!" program *exactly as shown* and try running it.

3 Modify your program so that it outputs the phrase "C++ is EASY!" instead.

4 Move the "\n" at the end of the message to somewhere in the middle (e.g. "Hello,\nWorld!") and re-run the program. Hence deduce what the character sequence "\n" is used for.

02

handling data

In this chapter you will learn

- how to store data in memory
- how to perform arithmetic
- how to print messages on the screen
- how to get data from the user

Aims of this chapter

In this chapter we will discuss one of the most important topics in programming: the input and output of data. You will learn how to store various kinds of information in memory, how to perform simple operations on it, and how to move it between the computer and the user.

2.1 Physical memory

At the simplest hardware level, computer memory chips are large banks of two-state circuits each capable of representing one binary digit – a one or a zero. This is the smallest possible quantity of storage space (being able to store only two different values) and it is called a *bit*. To the processor, a bit can have a value of one or zero, but to a program, it can represent any property that has two different states. Often, single bits are used as *flags*. A function might send back a string of eight bits, with the value of each having an independent meaning. When used as flags in this way, bits are often described as 'set' (=1) or 'clear' (=0).

The next named portion of memory is the *byte*. Each byte consists of eight bits, and can therefore store 256 (2 to the power of 8) different values. Bytes are significant because they are the basic division used by the central processor, which has two implications:

- There are no processor instructions that work on single bits, so to look at a bit, you must read in the entire byte.

- The memory addressing system counts bytes, not bits. This means that single bits cannot be pointed to by an address – you can only reference the byte which holds that bit.

Since the architecture of the processor makes working with bytes much easier and faster than working with individual bits, performance-conscious programmers sometimes use a whole byte even when a single bit would suffice. However, if memory use was at a premium, in a network communications program for example, data would be squeezed into the smallest possible unit of storage.

2.2 Interpreting stored data

Just like the bit, the byte's 256 values can be interpreted however the programmer chooses, the most common non-numeric use being for storing characters. Of course, in memory the contents is still just a collection of eight binary digits. When interpreted numerically, bytes can represent a value between 0 and 255 (when the byte is said to be *unsigned*), or between −128 and 127 (when the byte is said to be *signed*). Why the two different ranges? The answer is that there is no 'minus sign' facility built into the memory. To represent negative numbers, it is necessary to designate one of the bits the *sign flag*. If this bit is set, the remaining seven bits are to be interpreted as negative; if it is clear, the remaining seven are interpreted as positive. The very leftmost bit acts as the sign flag, which means that numbers from 00000000 to 01111111 (binary) are positive, and numbers from 10000000 to 11111111 (binary) are negative. In memory, you still just have a collection of eight bits, and there is no way of telling whether the byte you are looking at is supposed to represent an unsigned value, a signed value, an ASCII character, or some other object entirely. Fortunately, the rules governing memory allocation in C++ can help both programmer and compiler differentiate between the possibilities.

2.3 Allocating memory space in C++

To store values in a C++ program, you need to create one or more *variables*. A variable is a named object in memory that represents a known variety of data, depending on its intended use. C++ incorporates four basic variable types and a number of *type modifiers*, which are additional keywords that can be added to the declaration to give the compiler further information about how you intend to use these variables. The primitive data types are:

    char   one byte long, and enough to store one character.

    int   the general-purpose integer is two bytes long and can store values between −32,768 and 32,767.

    float   is used for floating-point numbers (fractions). It can store a number to seven significant figures of accuracy but it takes four bytes to do so.

double the largest of the primitives, a double takes eight bytes and can store floating-point numbers to fifteen significant digits of accuracy.

Although it would be possible to use a variable of type **double** in every situation, programs run faster and occupy less memory if you use the smallest variable that does the job.

The act of creating a variable is called *declaration*, because it involves *declaring* to the compiler that a certain name will represent a certain quantity and type of data. Once you have declared a variable, you can use it as many times as you like within the program code.

Variable declaration basic syntax:

    type name;

type is any C++ data type, 'name' is a unique user-defined name.

For example:

```
char letter;      // a single-byte variable called 'letter'
int number;       // an integer variable called 'number'
float fraction;   // a floating-point variable called 'fraction'
double big_frac;  // a double-precision variable called big_frac
```

Variable names are part of a larger group of user-defined names which are collectively termed *identifiers*. C++ identifiers are *always* case sensitive, and are restricted to the characters A to Z, a to z, 0 to 9, and underscore.

The first character of an identifier name must not, however, be a digit – this would confuse the compiler into seeing a number, rather than a name. Furthermore, be aware that certain names belong to the group of *reserved words* that, although perfectly legal in their own right, cannot be used to name variables because they already have a special meaning to the compiler. For example, you may not call a variable 'float' because that word already has special significance. Most compilers have a built-in code editor that automatically highlights keywords such as these in a different colour.

The program below shows the primitive types in use. The user is prompted to enter some data, which is then printed back onto the screen afterwards. To achieve this, we need to introduce the counterpart to the **cout** function, which is called **cin**. This function handles the task of taking the user's keyboard input and converting it into stored program data, as is demonstrated below...

```cpp
/* input.cpp  (30/9/1999)
Simple I/O Demonstration */

#include <iostream.h>

int main()
{
    // declare some variables
    char character;
    int integer;
    float fraction;
    double doublefraction;

    // prompt the user for input
    cout << "Please enter a character...";
    cin >> character;

    cout << "Now an integer number...";
    cin >> integer;

    cout << "Now a decimal fraction...";
    cin >> fraction;

    cout << "And another...";
    cin >> doublefraction;

    // display the results
    cout << "\nYou entered:";
    cout << "\nThe character " << character;
    cout << ", and the numbers "<< integer << ", " << fraction;
    cout << " and " << doublefraction << "\n";

    // exit
    return 0;
}
```

Notice the short single-line comments that explain what is happening at each point in the code.

First, four **cin** statements are used to get input from the user. The function is clever enough to perform the correct interpretation depending on the type of variable specified by the >> [**name**] part of the statement. The results are displayed on the screen by separating normal double-quoted strings of text and actual variable names with the << symbols. Although four lines are used to improve readability, it would be perfectly possible to produce the entire output of the program with just one long **cout** statement, listing each variable name and the adjoining strings in sequence. A test run looks like this:

```
Please enter a character...a
Now an integer number...20
Now a decimal fraction...1.5
And another...0.7
You entered:
The character a, and the numbers 20, 1.5 and 0.7.
```

Since we have not included any error-handling code, the program will crash out immediately if it encounters any problems; try typing letters instead of digits for the integer and see what happens!

2.4 Assignment and arithmetic operators

Now that basic input and output has been covered, it's time to start thinking about a program that might actually make use of the entered data. This next portion of code introduces some simple mathematical operations as well as demonstrating more advanced use of variables.

In C++, a lot of data manipulation is achieved not with functions, but with operators. Operators are usually represented by one or more symbolic characters and perform a wide range of tasks, including basic arithmetic, numerical comparison and Boolean logic. As your code becomes more complex, the simple jobs performed by these operators might become less useful in their own right, but you will find they still play a big role in any kind of loop or conditional program structure.

There are three important words associated with the use of operators:

- An *identifier* is any collection of letters and numbers that represents, or identifies, some object in memory. It is usually the name of a variable.

- An *operand* is the entity that an operator operates on. Some operators use two operands, one each side of the operator symbol; others use only one. It could be a single identifier, a constant, or a collection of other identifiers and operators.

- An *expression* is any collection of identifiers, operators and constants that, when evaluated (worked out) by the program, give some result. This result can then be incorporated into further expressions. The simplest expression is a constant number, e.g. 10; a more complex one would be (A + 10)/B. Note that in the second example, the parentheses determine the order in which the sub-expressions are evaluated before the final result is calculated.

The assignment operator = is probably the most used of all. Without it, it would be very difficult to accomplish anything, because there would be no simple way to assign a value to a variable. It is used like this:

identifier = expression

Remember, an identifier is a name that represents any writable object. The expression is made up of any number of names, numbers and operators combined so that they result in a value suitable for storage in the identifier variable. Common sense will tell you what you can use where; if you can't do it with a calculator, the chances are that the compiler will refuse to do it.

Now for the arithmetic operators, which are used in the next program:

+ Addition
− Subtraction
* Multiplication
/ Division
% Modulus (remainder)
++ Increment (add one)
-- Decrement (subtract one)

The increment/decrement operators are included in the language because these operations are so commonly used, even in very low-level programs, that it makes sense to have a special operator. In fact, most computer processors actually have their own separate increment/decrement instructions; they are usually around three times as fast as the equivalent addition/subtraction operation. You will see them come into their own in Chapter 4.

The code below shows the arithmetic operators in action. We will also be using *type modifiers* – additional keywords that are employed in conjunction with the primitive data types to adjust various aspects of their behaviour. You will see that variables can be initialized with a certain value when they are declared. If a variable is not initialized, its content is undefined, because it simply picks up the value of whatever data most recently occupied that memory space. You should never rely on the value of an uninitialized variable being zero, even though it often is…

```cpp
/* arith.cpp (30/9/1999)
Arithmetic Operators Demo */

#include <iostream.h>

int main()
{
    // declare & initialize variables
    const float taxrate = 25.5;
    long int bankbalance = 1000000;
    unsigned int earnings = 0;
    // prompt user for some info
    cout << "Earnings this month?";
    cin >> earnings;

    // update the balance for this month
    bankbalance = bankbalance + (earnings * (100 - taxrate)/100);

    // print result and quit
    cout << "\nThe new balance is " << bankbalance;
    return 0;
}
```

Modifiers

There are three type modifiers in use here.

- First, the **const** modifier is used to fix the variable **taxrate** at its initial value – any attempt to change it will cause a compiler error.

- The **long** modifier instructs the compiler to allocate four rather than two bytes to the integer **bankbalance**. This extends its range from the –32,768 to +32,767 to a gigantic –2,147,483,648 to +2,147,483,647 — more than enough for most people, I hope.

- Finally, the **unsigned** modifier is used on the variable **earnings**, which I have optimistically assumed to be positive. This shifts its range from –32,768 to +32,767 to 0 to 65,536 so all the negative values are now being used to represent the additional positive ones.

The output looks something like this:

```
Earnings this month?800
The new balance is 1000600
```

The actual calculation is a complex expression which is separated into several sections by the parentheses. It works like this:

- The percentage of income retained is equal to 100 minus the percentage paid in tax, so a 25.5% rate, as we have here, yields a 74.5% net return.

- To calculate net income we multiply gross earnings by the rate of return and divide by 100 (as the rate is a percentage).

- The net income figure is added to the current bank balance. We update the stored value by reassigning this new value back to the bank balance variable.

The pattern of performing some kind of operation on a certain variable and then reassigning the new value back to it is a common one, and the C++ language provides a shortcut for this kind of situation. In the previous example, we added a value to the variable **bankbalance** by taking its original value, adding the result of the net income calculation, and assigning the final total back to **bankbalance**:

```
bankbalance = bankbalance + (earnings * (100 - taxrate)/100);
```

The general pattern is

```
variable1 = variable1 + value;
```

…and it is useful with many other operators as well, including subtraction, multiplication and division. The shortcut I mentioned comes in the form of the *compound assignment operators*, which simply convert the line above into the form

```
variable1 += value;
```

This shorter form has the same meaning as before, but is neater and more efficient, because the compiler needs only to interpret the name 'variable1' a single time. In general, the syntax for compound assignment operators is as follows:

compound assignment operator syntax:

(expr1 op= expr2) is equivalent to (expr1 = expr1 op expr2)

op is any of + - * / % ^ | & << >>

For example:

```
A *= B; // multiplies A by B and stores the result in A.

A -= B; // subtracts B from A and stores the result in A.

// does the same as the line in arith.cpp
bankbalance += (earnings * (100 - taxrate) / 100);
```

2.5 Casting

So far all the variables we have used have been declared as a certain type and then used exclusively as that type, and when we get on to functions, you will see that any data passed to a function also has to be of the correct type. This system is satisfactory around 90% of the time and is advantageous because it allows the compiler to catch many kinds of type-conflict errors before the program is even run. However, I have stressed that whatever a variable is supposed to represent, it is still the same old binary number in memory. Furthermore, a single bit holding the value 1 means the same to a human being as a long double holding 1 does. These factors are often important to the programmer and lead to the concept of *casting*.

Casting is a mechanism provided by the compiler to override much of the default type checking, and can be extremely useful when passing data to functions that expect a different type. Suppose, for example, that you are writing a program to draw pretty geometric patterns on the screen. You would want to keep the current X and Y positions in float or double variables, to maintain accuracy throughout your – presumably iterative – calculations. However, the screen is only accurate to integers because it is divided into pixel dots, so you cannot display, for example, 3.5

pixels. This would mean, quite sensibly, that a function designed to plot a pixel on the screen would expect X and Y coordinates to be sent as integers. Now you have a problem. The solution, of course, is to use casting. You keep the X and Y variables as type float or double, but when you pass them to the pixel plotting function, you *cast* them to integers, thus rounding them down to the next pixel.

The syntax for casting is simplicity itself – just put the variable name in brackets and add a type name to the front of the expression. In the example below, the floating-point variable **real** is cast to an integer using **int(real)**. Similarly, you could cast to a **char** using the expression **char(real)**.

```
/* casting.cpp (30/9/1999)
Casting floats to ints */

#include <iostream.h>
int main()
{
        // declare and initialize two arbitrary variables
        float real = 0;
        int approx = 0;

        // get a floating-point from the user
        cout << "Enter a float: ";
        cin >> real;

        // cast 'real' to an int and assign it to 'approx'
        approx = int(real);

        // output the results
        cout << "\nReal float is "<< real;
        cout << "\nRough int is " << approx;
        return 0;
}
```

Casting floats, doubles and long doubles to integers is risky for two reasons. First, any value outside the integer's –32,767 to +32,768 storage range will not be converted correctly, because the compiler simply ignores the higher-order bytes that make up the larger variable types. You should also bear in mind that fractional values are always rounded towards zero, because everything past the decimal point is discarded by the conversion process. Beware: this means that even for a value that is within the numerical range, a simple casting only gives the nearest integer around 50% of the time, as a test run will show:

```
Enter a float: 9.99

Real float is 9.99
Rough int is 9
```

The compiler does a lot of implicit casting for you when performing arithmetic involving two variables of a different type. If you try to multiply an integer by a double, for example, the compiler automatically converts the integer to a double *before* performing the calculation. Thus, in any expression involving a mixture of variable types, the result of the calculation will always have the same type as the most complex input. This mechanism is safe because the compiler always 'upgrades' the simpler type. The opposite conversion, changing a double down to an integer for example, would mean discarding some of the data. If this is definitely what you want, you can do so by explicitly casting either the inputs or the result of the expression down to whatever you need.

Summary

In this chapter you encountered your first fully-interactive programs. We covered the four basic data types in C++ (char, int, float, double) and some of the modifiers (unsigned, const, long) that you can use to customize them. The second example showed how to initialize variables with a given value when they are declared. You now know how to receive input from a user and return meaningful output.

You learnt about arithmetic operators and were introduced to the terms *identifier*, *operand* and *expression*. Finally, we looked at the implicit conversions used when working with two or more different variable types, and discussed how to override this behaviour with *casting*.

Exercises

1 Write a program that prompts the user for two integers, adds them, and prints the result.

2 Expand the first program so that it also displays the difference, product and quotient of the original pair of numbers. You will need to think about which variable types to use for storing the results.

3 Design and build a program that takes the radius of a circle as input, and then calculates and displays the corresponding diameter, circumference and area. It is worth defining a single variable at the start of the code to hold the value of pi.

03

decision making

In this chapter you will learn

- how to write decision-making programs
- how to compare two different values
- how to combine several tests

Aims of this chapter

This chapter introduces the **if** and **switch** statements, two special *control structures* which are used to direct the flow of the code depending on the results of logical comparisons. You will also meet a new set of operators, which are indispensable in dealing with this kind of structure.

3.1 The if statement

The days of simplistic start-to-finish programs are long gone; today, software is expected to be capable of performing one of a range of actions depending on a multitude of external factors, while still maintaining the utmost standards in user-friendly interfacing. This requirement necessitates a method for testing values and executing different code sections depending on the outcome, and the most basic form of such a mechanism is the **if** statement, which looks like this:

'if' statement syntax:

```
if (expression)
{
    statements;
    ...
}
```

or

```
if (expression)
{
    statements;
    ...
}
else
{
    statements;
    ...
}
```

Like most of the C++ keywords, the **if** statement is simple and logical to use. The expression on the first line can be anything that results in, or can be cast to, an integer value – a value of zero is interpreted as 'false' while any other value, including negatives, is interpreted as 'true'.

Statements to be performed if the expression is 'true' are grouped into a *code block* by a pair of {curly braces}. An optional further group of statements can be executed if the expression is 'false', using the **else** keyword. If only a single line of code – such as a function call – is to be executed after **if** or **else**, the curly braces are not required. The ellipsis (…) denotes further code that has been omitted for the sake of clarity.

3.2 Equality and relational operators

These operators are very often used as part of the expression inside the **if** statement, giving the programmer a great deal of control over what is happening in the code. These operators all return a simple 'true' or 'false' (non-zero or zero) value, depending on the values of their two operands. They are:

==	Equal to
!=	Not equal to
<	Less than
>	Greater than
<=	Less than or equal to
>=	Greater than or equal to

So, for example, you can test whether the value stored in one variable is equal to the value stored in another:

```
if (variable1 == variable2)
{
    // do something here
}
```

One of the hardest programming errors to spot is the use of a single = sign instead of a double one; in other words, using the assignment operator instead of the equality operator, thus:

```
if (variable1 = variable2)
{
    // spot the problem?
}
```

This kind of mistake can go unnoticed for a while because it is perfectly correct code, but it almost certainly won't have the effect you intended. When the computer reaches this part of the program, the value of **variable2** is assigned to **variable1**. The result of any assignment expression is always equal to the new value of the left-hand operand, so the code block will execute depending on the original value of **variable2**, *not* the comparison between the variables as in the first example. Get into the habit of double-checking *every* logical expression you write – you can save a great deal of debugging time later on!

3.3 Logical combination operators

Consider the following English sentences:

If I am over 18, and I can prove it, then I can buy alcohol.

If I want to do it, or I have to do it, then I will probably do it.

The key words here are 'and' and 'or' – they represent the two ways of combining a pair of logical statements. You can build similar compound expressions in C++ by using the logical combination operators && (AND) and || (OR). Using C++ syntax, those two example sentences might become:

```
if (over18 && proveit) { ... }
if (want || must) { ... }
```

...where **over18**, **proveit**, **want** and **must** are integer variables holding either non-zero or zero values to represent 'true' or 'false' (these are known as Boolean variables, after the mathematician George Boole). We can draw up a truth table of values for each of the logical combination operators, which shows the result of the expression depending on the value of each operand:

A && B (both A and B)		
A	B	OUT
true	true	true
true	false	false
false	true	false
false	false	false

A || B (either A or B)		
A	B	OUT
true	true	true
true	false	true
false	true	true
false	false	false

Using both types of operator together it is possible to check whether a value is within a certain given range, by first testing to see if it is above the lower boundary, and then testing to make sure it is below the upper boundary.

```
if ((age >= 13) && (age < 20))
{
    // we have a teenager between 13.0 and 19.99999
    ...
}
```

Notice how the result of each relational expression becomes an operand in the logical combination expression, which is then evaluated in the context of the if statement.

Simple **if** statements can also be written using the conditional operator, which is actually made up of the two characters ? and :. Although it makes for very succinct code, the conditional operator is often avoided where possible because **if** statements are easier to read. However, it can be useful when you need to include a simple conditional test in part of a larger complex expression – you'll see it in action later on.

conditional operator syntax:
```
logical expression ? expression1 : expression2
```

is equivalent to
```
if (logical expression) expression1;
else expression2;
```

The result of the whole statement is expression1 if the logical expression evaluates true, and expression2 if the logical expression evaluates false. Expression1 and expression2 must evaluate to the same type.

Let's look at a brief example of the if statement in action:

```
/* iftest.cpp (30/9/1999) 'if' demo with
relational and combinational operators */
#include <iostream.h>
int main()
{
    // declare an integer 'age' and initialize to zero
    int age = 0;
    // prompt the user for his (her) age
    cout << "How old are you?";
```

```
cin >> age;
// basic 'if' construct
if ((age < 13) || (age > 110))
{
    // print message and return (quit)
    cout << "You are far too young or far too old; sorry!\n";
    // end the program early
    return -1;
}
// if...else construct
if ((age >= 13) && (age < 17))
{
    cout << "Teenager, but too young to drive:\n";
    cout << "You have " << 17 - age << " years to go.\n";
}
else
{
    cout << "You are old enough to drive.\n";
    // single statement; no need for { and }
    if (age >= 55) cout << "...and you are probably old
enough to retire.\n";
}
    return 0;
}
```

The program prompts users for their age and prints different messages for different numeric ranges. The output looks something like this:

```
How old are you?18
You are old enough to drive.
```

Note the use of the line 'return −1;' within the first if block. This statement causes the main function, and hence the program, to end immediately. It is good practice to use a different return value for each different exit point – this gives both the operating system and the programmer information about the program's state at termination. Conventionally, programs return zero to signal successful completion, and negative numbers to signal errors, although you can return any integer you want. The age condition tested in the above example does not really imply an error of any kind, but it is still a reason to abort the program early, so it's been given a value of −1. If there was a second exit point, we might use "return −2;", and so on.

The program flow is simple enough to follow, but what you should realize here is that it takes *several* successive **if** blocks to achieve the desired result. Real-world programs rely heavily on what one might call the "situational logic" of the code – in other words, the position of a certain statement with respect to previous ones:

```
cout << "You are old enough to drive.\n";
```

The line above appears in the final **else** clause of **iftest.cpp**. By its position in the **if...else** block, it can be inferred that the user's age is *not* between 13 and 16 – if it was, we would have printed the "Teenager, but too young to drive" message instead.

Unfortunately, this information alone does not necessarily make the printed statement about driving age correct, because the **else** clause is executed when **age** is greater than 17 *or* when **age** is less than 13. However, the fact that another **if** block appears before this one, testing for ages below 13 or above 110, gives us *additional* information about the value of the **age** variable. Thus, by combining the two separately-tested conditions that are needed to reach this point, we have specified an exact range for the **age** variable without testing for it explicitly. It is this kind of compound structure that allows even the most complex logical problem to be solved using just **if** and **else** clauses.

3.4 The switch statement

As an alternative to the **if** statement, C++ provides the **switch** keyword. As the name suggests, this control structure is used primarily for switching control from some central point to several other areas of the program. Consider the following block of code:

```
// get a keystroke for the menu system
char c = getch();

if (c == 'n')
{
    createnew();
    ...
}
else
    if (c == 'o')
```

```
{
    openfile();
    ...
}
else
    if (c == 's')
    {
        savefile()
        ...
    }
```

Although the intention of the code is simple – to execute a different set of statements depending on the value of c – the actual implementation is not ideal. The code declares a new char variable and initializes it with the value returned by the **getch** ('get character') function, and then sets about handling the different values.

Even with just three different possibilities (c = 'n', c = 'o', and c = 's') we already have an if statement nested inside an **if...else** statement nested inside another **if...else** statement – a better mechanism is needed, and here the switch statement becomes extremely useful.

'switch' statement syntax:

```
switch (integer expression)
{
case constant1:
    statements;
    ...
    break;
case constant2:
    statements;
    ...
    break;
...
default:
    statements;
    ...
}
```

The **switch** statement allows the programmer to create exactly the same structure as the one made of nested **if** statements discussed previously.

Notice:

- The expression in the first line of the structure gives the value to be used for comparison with each of the constants in the case labels. It must return an integer value.

- Control switches to the statement immediately after the **case** label whose constant matches the value of the integer expression given in the first line.

- If none of the constants match the value of the integer expression, control passes to the statement immediately following the **default:** tag. If no default tag is supplied, control passes to the statement immediately following the switch structure.

- A **break** statement normally appears at the end of each set of statements following a **case** label. This causes control to pass to the statement immediately following the **switch** structure, once the statements belonging to the given **case** label have executed. If omitted, control passes to whatever statement was below it, *even if that statement is inside a new case label.* Occasionally, this feature can be very useful, but omission of the **break** is also another favourite mistake of novice C++ programmers.

Since **switch** only works with integer expressions, you may be surprised to see the use of the letters 'n', 'o' and 's' in the code sample below. Using them in this way is legal because in C++, a character enclosed in single quotes represents a numeric ASCII value. Thus, what the switch statement is *actually* doing is a comparison of single-byte integers; the fact that each number represents a particular human-readable character is of no consequence here. The previous example, which tested for c == 'n', c == 'o' and c == 's', could be re-written like this:

```
char c = getch();

// the (c) means that it is the value of
// c  that is compared with 'a', 'n', 'o', etc.
switch (c)
{
case 'n':  // arrive here if c == 'n'
    createnew();
    ...
    break; // don't continue on to case 'o'
```

```
case 'o':   // arrive here if c == 'o'
    openfile();
    ...
    break; // don't continue on to case 's'

case 's':   // arrive here if c == 's'
    savefile();
    ...
    break; // this one isn't strictly necessary

default: // arrive here if c is neither 'n', 'o' nor 's'.
    ...
    break;
}
```

The great thing about the **switch** statement is that the number of cases handled can increase almost indefinitely without any real increase in complexity. When you start writing software for Microsoft Windows, or indeed any event-driven operating system, you will find yourself using it a great deal – there is nearly always a long switch statement at the heart of every Windows program.

3.5 A stylistic taboo

A final word on the 'other' flow control keyword. Mainly to improve backwards compatibility rather than to encourage good programming practice, C++ includes a **goto** statement. If you have ever written anything in BASIC, or even an MS-DOS batch file, you will probably have come across it, but in case you haven't, here is the syntax:

'goto' statement syntax:

```
    goto identifier;
    statements;
    ...
identifier:
    statements;
    ...
```

On execution of the **goto** statement, control is *unconditionally* transferred to the statement marked by the identifier. Excessive use of **goto** is considered extremely bad programming practice, due to the fact that the jump is unconditional, and that control can be passed to *any* statement in the entire source code file. These mean that one soon ends up with difficult-to-maintain, bug-prone 'spaghetti code'. For example:

```
// check the value of i
if (i >= 0)
    // if i is not negative, go to 'next'
    goto next;
// otherwise reset i to zero.
i = 0;
next:
// continue execution...
DoSomething();
...
```

Even in this trivial section of code, things are already starting to get messy. It is not clear without reading above whether or not the "i =0;" statement is executed or not, and under what conditions. A *far* better way to write this section is given below:

```
if (i < 0) i = 0;
DoSomething();
```

...simpler, neater and more controlled. In fact – if you can manage it – you should aim *never* to use goto, but if it does come in useful, save it for 'emergencies' only.

Summary

In this chapter we discussed two important methods of directing the flow of your code – the **if** statement, which is used to make decisional jumps to different blocks of code, and the **switch** statement, which is used to vector between code sections depending on the value of an integer variable. We also covered the equality, relational and logical combination operators, which come in useful when writing expressions that control execution. You now have enough know-how to create quite sophisticated programs, capable of performing different tasks depending on the user's input.

Exercises

1 Using the listing of **iftest.cpp** in this chapter as a basis, write a program that can differentiate between childhood, teen, middle and old age having prompted the user for his/her age.

2 Create a version of the old number guessing game. Users enter a number and get feedback – "too high", "too low", "close", "very close" etc. – until they guess right. For now, design it so that the user must re-run the program for each attempt. You could define the target number as a **const** variable.

3 Write a program that gets a character from the user and categorizes it into lowercase letter, uppercase letter, number or other. You can make use of the fact that each of these groups have consecutive ASCII codes; the digit characters are within codes 48 to 58, for instance.

4 Expand the circle calculator program from the Chapter 2 exercises so that the user can enter *either* the radius, diameter, circumference or area of a circle, and get the other three figures back from the program. You will need to ask the user which one of the four possible dimensions they want to enter, before prompting them for the actual value.

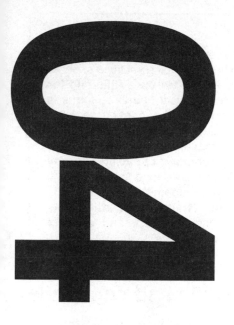

04

iterative programs

In this chapter you will learn

- how to create looping blocks of code
- how to build lists and tables of data
- how to work with strings of characters

Aims of this chapter

This chapter covers another extremely important aspect of flow control – the ability to create looping sections of code. In C++, this is handled by the **while**, **do...while** and **for** keywords; the only difference between the three forms is *when* the condition that decides whether or not to redo the loop is tested. Repeated blocks of statements are important in programming because computers derive much of their worth from their number-crunching capability, so any program designed to work through a long list of data will involve some kind of iterative (looping) behaviour. It is appropriate, then, that this chapter also introduces techniques for creating and managing lists and tables of variable data through the use of *arrays*.

4.1 Loops with while and do...while

The simplest structure is the **while** loop, which has the same basic layout as an **if** construct – a keyword, a logical expression, and a block of statements:

'while' statement syntax:

```
while (expression)
{
    statements;
    ...
}
```

For as long as the logical expression is 'true', i.e. non-zero, the block of statements executes. When the last statement has completed, control passes back to the first. Unless you plan to create an infinite loop, at least one of the statements in the block should affect the outcome of the test expression in some way. For example:

```
char c = 0;

// this loop keeps repeating until c equals 32
while (c != 32)
{
    ...
```

```
    statements;
    ...
    c = getch();
}
```

The conditional expression shown above makes use of the != operator which has the translation 'not equal to'. If the variable **c** is not equal to 32, the result of the expression **c** != **32** is 'true' and the loop continues. If **c** *is* 32, the expression **c** != **32** evaluates to 'false' and the loop stops. Thus, when the **getch** function returns the ASCII code 32 (space) the program will continue to the end of the statement block and then go on to the first line after the closing curly brace.

An alternative to the **while** loop is the **do...while** structure. Like the simple **while** loop, the block is repeatedly executed for as long as the logical expression is true. This time however, the block is executed *before* the expression is evaluated, which means that regardless of the logical expression, the code within the loop will always execute once.

'do...while' statement syntax:

```
do
{
    statements;
    ...
} while (logical expression);
```

Choosing between a **while** loop or a **do...while** loop is simply a case of deciding whether the test expression should be evaluated *before* or *after* the loop body is executed each time. Be aware that while most tasks could be coded using either structure, there are cases where this distinction is very important.

4.2 For, break and continue

The third variety of looping structure is created using the **for** keyword. Although the operation performed by **for** *could* be coded using a while loop, this method is both neater and more efficient.

'for' statement syntax:

```
for (expression1; expression2; expression3)
```

```
{
    statements;
    ...
}
```

Expression1 is evaluated when control first passes to this structure.

The block of statements is continually executed until *expression2* becomes false.

With every iteration through the loop, *expression3* is also evaluated.

The meaning of this code can be easily explained by demonstrating its exact functional equivalent using a **while** loop, which is shown below.

```
expression1;
while (expression2)
{
    statements;
    ...
    expression3;
}
```

Evidently, the **for** version is neater, and easier to read – once you know what it means. However, one small error that can cause a difficult-to-spot and probably serious bug in your program is the addition of a semicolon after the **for** line. This would cause the program to loop through a blank statement however many times, and then to execute the main statement block only once. Although it will be obvious that something is wrong, you may have great difficulty finding the error – it is very easy to overlook this simple typo.

Instead of a simple statement, you can also put a variable declaration into *expression1* of a **for** loop – this saves having to declare a suitable counting variable at the start of the program. For example:

```
for(int i = 0; i < 10; i++) { ... }
```

creates a section of code that loops ten times. Note that the variable i continues to exist even outside the loop structure where it was declared.

Another interesting feature of the **for** loop's syntax is that all three expressions are optional. If the first or the third is omitted, no expression is executed in that place. When the second is omitted, it is automatically evaluated as true, so the block of statements is still executed. A simple way of creating an infinite loop, then, is to code the following:

```
for (;;)
{
    statements;
    ...
}
```

break

The statements between the curly braces are executed continuously; the loop only stops when the program is ended. Only? Not quite. C++ includes another keyword designed specifically to break out of structures using the **while**, **do...while**, and **for** statements. It is called, unsurprisingly, **break**, and has already appeared as part of the **switch** structure (page 31). In the infinite **for** loop given above, the code might execute a **break** to pass control to the next statement after the loop:

```
for (;;)
{
    ...

    // break out if necessary; otherwise, execution continues
    if (some expression) break;
    ...
}
// arrive here if the break is executed
...
```

While particularly significant within infinite loops, the **break** keyword can also be useful within the more usual style of repeating structure – for example, to stop the loop half way through the block of statements.

continue

There is also an exact opposite to the **break** keyword. While **break** passes control to the next statement after the end of a control structure, **continue** passes control back to the beginning. Such a feature can be used to skip loop iterations if a certain condition occurs. For example:

```
while (some expression)
{
    ...

    // skip back to the top if necessary
    if (some other expression) continue;

    // otherwise just keep going
    ...
}
```

Keep it in mind that when the computer encounters a **continue** statement within a **for** structure, that third expression is still evaluated before the body of the loop is restarted.

Here's an example program that demonstrates the use of the **for** and **break** keywords, as well as introducing a new way to create variables.

As the first line of the **main** function shows, you can declare several variables of the same type by separating their names with commas. This style avoids needless repetition of the type name, and if it's several **const unsigned long ints** that you're after, that can mean quite a saving on typing. Here, the integers **account**, **code** and **i** are all declared at the same time with the line **int account, code, i;**.

```
/* loops.cpp (30/9/1999)
Using for and break statements */

#include <iostream.h>

int main()
{
    // declare some integers
    int account, code, i;

    // allow three login attempts
    for (i = 0; i < 3; i++)
    {
        cout << "Account Number:";
        cin >> account;
```

```
cout << "PIN Code:";
cin >> code;
// break out of loop if code OK
if (code == 1234)
{
    cout << "\nLogin complete!";
    break;
}

// otherwise, try again
cout << "\n\nAccess denied: " << 2 - i << " attempt(s)
    left.\n";
}

// arrive here after either success, or three failures
return 0;

}
```

The output should look something like this:

```
Account Number:12345678
PIN Code:1234
Login complete!
```

4.3 Arrays

The loop constructs are particularly useful when you want to work with a list or a table of values. To accomplish this, you can use a variable array. The array mechanism provides a way of managing several similar values, rather than declaring separate variables for each object. Each element of the array is accessed by an index number, with zero for the first element. For more complex structures, multidimensional arrays are possible, but the basic syntax remains the same.

one-dimensional array
list[0]
list[1]
list[2]
list[3]
list[4]

two-dimensional array	
table[0][0]	table[0][1]
table[1][0]	table[1][1]
table[2][0]	table[2][1]
table[3][0]	table[3][1]
table[4][0]	table[4][1]

uninitialized array declaration syntax:

```
type name[size];
type name[dimension1][dimension2]...[dimensionN];
```

For example:

```
int quizmarks[30];
float hours[24][7];
```

initialized array declaration syntax:

```
type name[size] = {value1, value2, ... valueN};
type name[] = {value1, value2, ... valueN};
type name[dimension1]...[dimensionM] =
    { {value11, value12, ... value1M},
      {value21, value22, ... value2M},
      {valueN1, valueN2, ... valueNM} ... };
```

For example:

```
float results[] = {1.21, 3.412, -98.19};
char table[2][3] = { { 'A', 'B', 'C' }, { 'a', 'b', 'c' } };
```

Accessing array elements:

```
name[index] = expression;
name[index1][index2]...[indexN] = expression;
```

For example:

```
quizmarks[14] = 8;
```

Although the pure syntax is made to look complicated by the possibility of unlimited dimension tables, arrays are actually very easy to use. When declared, the size of the array goes in [square brackets]. For a two-dimensional array (a table) you simply specify two sets of brackets rather than one. To access a particular element you put the appropriate index number in the square brackets, as in the last example. Don't forget that the first element is [0] not [1]!

The array becomes an even more powerful tool when the *index* (the element number in the brackets) is specified not by a literal number but by the value of another variable, e.g. **quizmarks[count] = 10;** which would set the element corresponding to **count** to 10. If **count** counted the number of passes through a loop of code, each successive element of **quizmarks** could be set to some value. Any expression that results in an integer type can be used as an array index, but you must be careful: C++ will not automatically check that the index is within the declared range. If you specify an index number that is larger than the size of the array, you will overwrite memory allocated to other variables with possibly disastrous consequences.

4.4 Handling strings in C++

An interesting characteristic of C++ and its predecessor, C, is that there is no variable to hold strings. A string is any collection of characters (bytes) intended to be read as text by a human rather than as numbers by a computer, and most languages have a variable type designed to store such an object. C++ gives the programmer more flexibility by simply using an array of characters as a string. Because there is no set length for a piece of text, a *null character* – a byte with value zero – is used to mark the end of a string. Storing strings in this way makes it extremely easy to work through strings character-by-character for a certain sequence, because each successive increment of the array index is equivalent to moving along to the next character. However, it means that you cannot assign a string literal such as "Hello World!" straight to a string variable because the string variable is really just an array of bytes. These fragments outline declaration of a character array as a string.

```
// the long way... (notice the terminating null)
char message1[] = {'H', 'e', 'l', 'l', 'o', ',', ' ', 'W', 'o', 'r', 'l', 'd', '!', '\0'};

// the short way – the array size is determined automatically
char message2[] = "Hello World!";

// THIS WILL CAUSE A COMPILER ERROR
message1 = "Good Morning.";
```

The third statement causes a compiler error because the only time a string literal can be directly assigned to a char array is during initialization. To copy a literal string into a character array during the progam's execution requires the use of one of the *standard library functions* discussed later on.

There is an important difference between the two styles of quotes. Text surrounded by "double quotes" is interpreted as a *string literal*, and has a terminating null character automatically appended to it. Single letters surrounded by 'single quotation marks' are interpreted as the numerical ASCII value of that character. Thus 'A' is a single char byte with the value 65, but "A" means a two-element character array, with the first byte set to 65 and the second to zero.

There are a number of special *escape sequences* that can be used in string literals or as single characters, which include the '\0' in the first example. These codes allow special characters to be included when typing them directly would be difficult or ambiguous in meaning.

The escape sequences	
\a	Bell
\\	Backslash
\b	Backspace
\r	Carriage return
\"	Double quotation mark
\f	Form feed
\n	New line
\0	Null
\'	Single quotation mark
\t	Tab
\v	Vertical tab

So the literal string **"There are lots of \'.exe\' files\nin\t\"C:\\DOS\\\""** would actually fill a character array or be printed on the screen as:

```
There are lots of '.exe' files
in   "C:\DOS\"
```

The most important one to remember is \\ instead of just \. If you are specifying the drive and path for some file in a literal string, and you leave out the second backslash, the compiler will interpret the first backslash and the character after it as a completely different escape sequence – this is bound to seriously confuse the program!

You already know how to refer to a single element of an array, but especially when dealing with strings, you also need to refer to the entire array at once. For example, to print the string **message1** on the screen, you can use:

```
cout << message1;
```

The name of the array without any square brackets actually represents a special kind of variable, called a *pointer*, that holds the memory address of the first element of the array. So, when a function like **cout** needs to take a string as one of its arguments, what it actually gets is a pointer-to-char variable. Chapter 9 expands on this concept; it turns out that array notation is actually a kind of shorthand for accessing data via its numeric memory address. For now though, all you need to remember is that when passing a string to another function, you should just use the name of the array without brackets.

```
/* arrays.cpp (30/9/1999)
handling strings as arrays */

#include <iostream.h>
int main()
{
    // declare a fifty-character string and an integer
    char name[50]; int i;

    // prompt the user and get the name
    cout << "What's your name?";
    cin >> name;

    // work through up to 50 letters
    for (i = 0; i < 50; i++)
    {
        // stop if we get to the end
        if (!name[i]) break;
        // maybe print a hyphen, then the letter
        cout << (i ? "-" : "") << name[i];
    }

    // print last message and quit
    cout << "\nThat name is " << i << " letters long.\n";
    return 0;
}
```

Some of the aspects of string handling are demonstrated above. As before, the line **cin >> name;** does all the work in getting data from the user; notice how the name of the array without brackets is used to refer to the string as a whole. The program then enters a loop so that it can work through each character in turn, using the variable **i**, which counts the number of passes through the loop, to decide which character to operate on. This technique is extremely common – the counting variable of a 'for' loop is used as the index number of each character element within a string.

On the first pass through the loop body, **i** is zero and so **name[i]** is the same as **name[0]**, which is the first character of the string. On the next pass, **i** is one, and so **name[i]** gives us the second character of the string, and so on. When **name[i]** is zero, we have reached the null character that marks the end, and the value of **i** is equal to the total number of characters in the string.

In this example, the check for the null character is done straight away. This task is performed using the *logical negation operator* (an exclamation mark), which is used like the English word 'not'.

```
if (!name[i]) break;
```

Thus, if **name[i]** is non-zero (true), **!name[i]** evaluates to false. In the same way, if **name[i]** is zero (false), **!name[i]** is true and the **if** statement executes the **break** to end the loop.

In general:

logical negation operator syntax:

!(expression) returns the logical inverse of (expression)

For example:

if (!(A==B)) i.e. "if it is not true that A equals B"

is the same as

if (A!=B) i.e. "if A does not equal B"

The logical negation operator is often used in situations where some value must be compared with zero. Although code of the form 'if (**value** == 0) { ... }' is perfectly legal, most programmers prefer to use 'if (!**value**) { ... }' because it is shorter, and often seems to convey the purpose of the statement better – especially if you read the line as 'if *not* value, then ...'.

```
cout << (i ? "-" : "") << name[i];
```

The second statement prints the current character and a hyphen where necessary. The program's output looks a little like this:

```
What's your name?Richard
R-i-c-h-a-r-d
That name is 7 letters long.
```

Where necessary? The conditional operator, which was briefly mentioned in the section on **if** statements, really comes into its own here:

```
(i ? "-" : "")
```

If i is zero, as it is in the first time through the loop, the expression returns a blank string "" so that the first character doesn't have a hyphen in front of it. In subsequent iterations, i is non-zero so the logical expression evaluates to true and the conditional operator returns the string "-". This whole chunk can be included directly in a call to **cout**. The alternative, a conventional **if...else** construct, would mean testing the value of i and then making a different call to **cout** depending on the value:

```
if (i == 0)
    cout << name[i];
else
    cout << "-" << name[i];
```

Clearly, the conditional operator is a far neater solution here.

Summary

This chapter has covered the three ways of creating loop structures in C++ and has also discussed the **break** and **continue** keywords which are used for controlling program flow still further. Iterative code is especially useful when dealing with arrays, which you now know how to declare, initialize and access. Remember that strings in C++ are handled as character arrays, so the name of the string on its own is actually an address pointer to the first element. The use of arrays for strings explains why the compiler sees a difference between "a" and 'a'. In the last example, you saw the logical negation operator and the conditional operator in use for the first time, as two further ways of writing state-sensitive programs.

Exercises

1 Prompt the user for a number, and then print that many asterisks on the screen.

2 Write a program that counts from 1 to 100, printing each number on the screen.

3 Use a char array to store the user's name and then print a personalized greeting.

4 Write a program that encodes a string by converting a to b, b to c and so on (i.e. add one to each character in turn). Preserve any spaces and tabs.

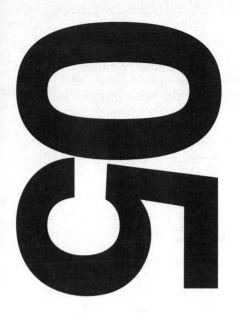

05

structured coding

In this chapter you will learn

- how to organize and
  modularize your programs
- how to assemble variables
  into functional groups
- how to create shortcuts and
  aliases for often-used code

Aims of this chapter

As your programs grow in size and complexity, it becomes more and more important to impose structure onto the code. This chapter introduces *functions*, *structures* and *unions*, which allow the programmer to group code and data into efficient, self-contained units. We will also look at *enum* and *typedef*, two keywords that can make projects easier to handle by assigning simpler, more convenient names to frequently-used constants and types.

5.1 Declaring a function

Functions allow a symbolic name to be attached to a convenient, modular block of code; this name is then used whenever that piece of code is to be executed. Although it is not compulsory, almost all functions either take starting parameters and/or return data. Consider the line of code below:

```
x = sqrt(y);
```

A function called **sqrt** is being run (*called*) with the aim of calculating the square root of **y** and storing it in **x**. The variable **y**, which must be of the correct type, is an *argument* – a piece of data that is passed to the function for it to do some kind of operation on. When the function ends, it is the *return value* that will be stored in the variable **x**, which must also be of compatible type.

Like variables, functions must be declared before they can be called. The declaration for a function must be repeated in every file where it is used, but the *definition*, which is where the body of the function is written out, only appears once. The declaration is usually given at the start of the program:

function declaration syntax:

```
type name(type arg1, type arg2, ...);
```

The various components of the declaration each supply the compiler with information about the function. The very first **type** gives the type of the data to be returned by the function.

If the function does not return anything, you must still use the keyword **void**. A complete list of the arguments to be passed to the function follows the function name, in parentheses. It is the *type* of each argument that is important here; the names can differ from the actual implementation of the function or can be omitted altogether. However, it is good coding practice to include the names that you will use later on – it improves readability and serves as a reminder of the function's details.

Here are some examples of function declarations:

```
void func1(void);        // no arguments, no return value
void func2();    // same thing as before
int func3();        // no arguments, returns an integer
// 3 arguments, returns a float
float func4(int num, char c, char k);
// again, 3 arguments, returns a float
float func5(int, char, char);
```

5.2 Defining a function

Once the function has been declared it can be called from anywhere in the program, but at some point the actual body must be defined. This part is known as the *definition* or *implementation* of the function.

function definition syntax:

```
type name(type arg1, type arg2, ...)
{
    statements;
    ...
    return type;
}
```

The first line of the definition is almost identical to the declaration. In this instance, the names of the arguments are important because you will have to refer to them in the body of the function.

A common error to watch for is the inclusion of a semicolon after this first line of the function definition; there should not be one.

The lines of code that make up the function itself are surrounded by {curly braces}, and the function ends after the last line of code, or whenever a **return** statement is encountered. The **return** specifies what value is returned to the calling function (i.e. the section of code that made the jump to this function). The value returned could be a hard-coded number, or it could be the contents of a variable, but it must always have the same type as that declared in the function declaration and at the beginning of the function definition. In anything other than a void function, there must always be a **return** at the very end, or the compiler will raise an error. However, you can use additional **return** statements at any point within the body code as a way of ending the function immediately.

5.3 Functions in action

The program listed below demonstrates the use of a simple user-defined function, and also creates the opportunity to discuss another fresh handful of minor language elements...

```
/* function.cpp (30/9/1999)
functions and global variables */

#include <iostream.h>

// declare the calc() function and a constant float
int calc(float radius);
const float pi = 3.145927f;

int main()
{
    float input;
    int ok;

    // print welcome message
    cout << "Circle Calculator: Enter zero to quit.";
    cout << "\n(approximating pi to " << pi << ")";

    do
    {
        // prompt for circle radius
        cout << "\nEnter radius?";
        cin >> input;
```

```
        // stop the loop if necessary
        if (cin.fail()) break;

        // call calc() to print results
        ok = calc(input);

    // loop if calc() returned true
    } while (ok);

    return 0;
}

// calculate diameter, circumference, area, and print results
int calc(float radius)
{
    // declare locals and check input value
    float area, diameter, circumference;
    if (radius <= 0) return 0;

    // calculate the values
    diameter = radius * 2;
    circumference = pi * diameter;
    area = radius * radius * pi;

    // output results and return 'true'
    cout << "area = " << area << ", diameter = " << diameter;
    cout << ", circumference = " << circumference << "\n";
    return 1;
}
```

I suggest you compile and run this one before going further, to get the feel of the program and what it does.

A test run looks like this:

```
Circle Calculator: Enter zero to quit.
(approximating pi to 3.145927)
Enter radius?10
area = 314.592682, diameter = 20, circumference = 62.918541

Enter radius?0
```

Let's look at some of the important features:

```
int calc(float radius);
```

The first line of code is a declaration for the function that we will use later. As you can see, the function is called **calc**, it has one floating-point argument, and it returns an integer value. Although the name **radius** can be left out, it is good programming practice to include it because it helps to remind a reader what the argument is for.

```
const float pi = 3.145927f;
```

The next line is a normal variable declaration, except that it appears outside any function block. This makes it a global variable – one which is accessible from any part of the source code. Since both the **main** function and the **calc** function use the variable **pi**, it must be declared this way. The letter 'f' on the end of the number tells the compiler that '3.1415927' is a float, not a double. This is useful because some compilers will issue a warning when you try to assign what looks like an eight-byte constant to a four-byte floating-point variable; others will perform the conversion without complaining. In a similar way, you can add 'L' to the end of a number to make it represent a long (four-byte) integer constant, rather than a short (two-byte) one.

The next point of interest is the **do…while** loop at the centre of the program:

```
do
{
    cout << "\nEnter radius?";
    cin >> input;
    if (cin.fail()) break;
    ok = calc(input);
} while (ok);
```

The third line of the block tests whether or not the previous **cin** statement was successful. This is important because a user could enter, for example, a letter instead of a number at the prompt, confusing the input mechanism and causing the program to run into an infinite loop. To prevent this, we call the **cin.fail()** function, which returns a true or false value depending on whether the most recent input operation was successful. If the integer input failed, we break the loop immediately.

Assuming the variable input now contains a valid integer, we call our **calc** function to determine the corresponding area, diameter and circumference and output the result. If you look at the definition of **calc** you will see that it returns zero or one depending on the value of the argument **radius**, which in this case is a copy of the variable input in **main**. If the argument is invalid, **calc** is ended immediately by the line:

```
if (radius <= 0) return 0;
```

Otherwise, execution continues up to the final **return 1;** statement. This return code is stored in the variable **ok**, so for as long as **calc** returns true, the loop continues to run. If the user enters zero, **calc** returns false and the loop stops. This arrangement is a common one – functions are often designed to return a Boolean value to indicate success or failure.

5.4 Data scope

As you saw with **float pi** in the last example, the lifetime of a variable, and its accessibility by functions, depends on where it is declared within the source file.

- Variables declared outside any function are called *global* variables, and are said to have global or file-level scope. This means that they are accessible and modifiable from any function within the source file. Global variables are allocated when the program begins, exist throughout its runtime, and are destroyed only when the program ends.

- Variables declared inside a function are called *local* or automatic variables. A local variable is accessible only from within the function that declares it, and is normally created and then destroyed each time the function is called. The declaration can be modified with the **static** type modifier, which ensures that local variables maintain their value between calls to the function. Such a variable is useful for storing data that depends on a previous call to the same function. If you add an initializing value to the declaration of a static variable, it will only be initialized the first time the function is called; during subsequent calls the variable will have whatever value it was left with following the previous time around.

The novice programmer is often tempted to make every variable global, in the name of simplicity. While this may hold true for small programs, larger projects will quickly become cluttered and unmanageable if every variable is made global. There is also the danger that since global data can be modified from any point in the file, bug-tracking and development will become progressively more complicated. It is better programming style to make as few variables global as possible – a more structured approach will reduce the possibility of fatal bugs and make maintaining the code easier.

A final feature of scope is that global variables are always masked by local equivalents. Thus, if a function argument or local variable has the same name as a global one, regardless of its type, any reference to that name will always apply to the local copy. To access the global version of a variable that is masked by a local variable of the same name, the scope resolution operator :: is used. Remember though that if you have nested levels of local scopes, the scope resolution operator still goes straight to the global instance of the named variable.

```cpp
/* scope.cpp (30/9/1999)
static variables and :: operator */

#include <iostream.h>

// global declarations
int count;
void printmessage();

int main()
{
    // modify the global version of count
    count = 100;
    printmessage();

    // modify the global version again
    count = 200;
    printmessage();

    return 0;

}

void printmessage()
{
    // static local variable with name clash
    static int count = 0;

    // print our own local version first, then the global one
```

```
cout << "Local int count is " << count << "\n";
cout << "Global int count is " << ::count << "\n";

// increment the local version of count
count++;
}
```

Here we see the :: operator and the static modifier in use. The first call to the **printmessage** function initializes the *local* version of **count** to zero and gets a value of 100 from the *global* version of **count**. After printing these values, the function increments the local count with the statement **count++**. When **printmessage** is called a second time, the *local* **count** has the value of 1 that it ended up with last time around, and the *global* **count** now has a value of 200 because it was modified by the **main** function before the second call. Here's the output:

```
Local int count is 0
Global int count is 100
Local int count is 1
Global int count is 200
```

If you delete the **static** keyword and re-run the program, you will see that the local **count** gets re-initialized to zero each time **printmessage** is called.

5.5 Structuring data

Just as there are ways of organizing segments of code into functions, loops and conditional structures, so there are several ways to manage and control a program's data. In the following examples, the basic types **char**, **int**, **float** and **double** still actually allocate memory, but their functionality is combined and enhanced by four new keywords: **typedef**, **enum**, **struct** and **union**.

typedef

typedef is used to define new data types. Treat that word 'new' with caution; **typedef** does not allow the creation of a completely new kind of variable, it merely allows the programmer to define synonyms for existing compound types. **typedef** statements are generally placed at the top of the source file, so they appear before any code that uses them.

typedef syntax:

    typedef type name;

The statement simply makes *name* a synonym for *type*. By convention, names created using **typedef** are put into upper case to avoid confusion with the names of variables and functions. For example,

    typedef const unsigned long int ULONG;

makes the line

    ULONG Number = 3001;

exactly equivalent to

    const unsigned long int Number = 3001;

Clearly, **ULONG** is much more convenient than **const unsigned long int** – adding a few **typedef** statements early in a program's development can save you a lot of typing! By using the synonym **ULONG**, the programmer also ensures that all of the necessary type modifiers are included, rather than trying to remember them each time.

enum

You can use **enum** to define a set of named integer constants, called *enumerators*, in an appropriate group. Although the compiler produces the same code whatever, you can use *enumerated types* like these to make your code easier to understand and maintain. Unless a specific initializer is given, the first constant has value zero; the second, one; the third, two; and so on. Identifiers do not have to be unique; by explicitly assigning values, you can force several to have the same value.

enum syntax:

    enum name
    {
        identifiers [= values],
        ...
    } [instances ...] ;

name	The name of the enumerated type
identifiers	Names of constants, with optional values
instances	Optional list of variables to declare

The syntax can look a little complicated at first, due mainly to the fact that many of the sections are optional or adaptable. The following example shows how the days of the week can be associated with integer values using an enumeration called **days**. Once the enumerated type has been defined, you can declare instances of it just as you would a normal variable:

```
/* enum.cpp (30/9/1999)
enumerated types demo */

#include <iostream.h>

// declare a new enumerated type 'days'
enum days
{
    Saturday, // Saturday = 0 by default
    Sunday = 0, // Force Sunday = 0 as well
    Monday,     // Monday = 1 (Sunday + 1)
    Tuesday, // Tuesday = 2
    Wednesday, // Wednesday = 3
    Thursday,// etc.
    Friday
} today; // declare a new variable 'today' of type 'days'

int main()
{
    // declare two more 'days' objects
    days yesterday, tomorrow;

    // assign some values and print
    today = Tuesday;
    yesterday = today - 1;
    tomorrow = today + 1;
    cout << "Today is " << today;
    cout << "\nYesterday was " << yesterday;
    cout << "\nTomorrow will be " << tomorrow;
    return 0;
}
```

A test run produces this output:

```
Today is 2
Yesterday was 1
Tomorrow will be 3
```

The arithmetic is possible because enumerated types are just integers in disguise. Be aware that some compilers can be configured to store **enums** as **char** variables instead, if the initializers all fall within either the signed or the unsigned range. This halves the memory use but will cause problems at run-time if you expect to have two bytes at hand!

struct

struct is used to group variables into a single, identifiable structure. The size of a structure is given simply by adding the size of each component part – there is nothing hidden or unexpected.

struct syntax:

```
struct name
{
    declarations;
    ...
} [instances ...];
```

name   The name of the new structure

declarations   Declarations for data members

instances   Optional list of variables to declare

A new **struct** is defined in much the same way as a new **enum**, but here, normal variable declarations replace the list of constants. It is important to note that the declarations can *not* include initializers. The struct definition itself does not cause any memory to be allocated, so there would be nowhere to store the initial values that you specified. Once the struct has been defined you can declare new objects based on it, just as you would normal variables. It is this declaration statement that actually allocates memory.

```
/* struct.cpp (30/9/1999)
using the struct keyword */

#include <iostream.h>

// define a new structure
struct PERSON
```

```
{
    int     age;
    float   height;
    float   weight;
};

int main()
{
    // declare a instance of the 'PERSON' struct
    PERSON alex;

    // set the member variables
    alex.age = 12;
    alex.height = 1.42f;
    alex.weight = 40.0f;

    // output each member variable in turn
    cout << "Age: " << alex.age;
    cout << "\nHeight: " << alex.height;
    cout << "\nWeight: " << alex.weight;

    return 0;
}
```

Defining a new structure is as simple as giving it a name and
listing the variables that make up its contents. Once an instance
of the structure has been created, the stop mark . (dot) is used
to specify which member variable is being accessed. It is called
the *member selection operator*, and is used to separate the name
of the structure object from the name of the member variable
itself. For instance, **alex.age** and **alex.height** both refer to the
same instance of the structure, but to different member variables. The program output should look something like this:

```
Age: 12
Height: 1.42
Weight: 40
```

Occasionally, a programmer working with lower-level data
structures will need to ensure that each member of a C++ struct
starts at an even two-byte, four-byte, eight-byte or sixteen-byte
address boundary. Most compilers have a command line option
that modifies what is known as the *structure member alignment*
to achieve this; spare 'padding' bytes are inserted as necessary

between the members. You are unlikely to come across this feature unless you have – to quote Microsoft – 'specific alignment requirements'. However, it is worth knowing that it exists because under such conditions, it is no longer safe to assume that one member follows directly on from its predecessor.

union

A **union** is very like a structure, with one exception – all the members start at the same point in memory, rather than each being assigned their own space. Thus, the member variables effectively share the memory, which means that only one can be used at a time. The size of a union is given by the size of its largest member.

```
/* unions.cpp (30/9/1999)
using the union keyword */
#include <iostream.h>

// we'll use a simple function to print the values
void printdata();

// declare a union 'DATA' to hold any of three types
union DATA
{
    char  c;
    int   i;
    float f;
} var1;

int main()
{
    var1.c = 'a';  // use the char variable...
    printdata();

    var1.i = 50;   // overwrite it with the integer
    printdata();

    var1.f = 2.98f;        // overwrite it with the float
    printdata();

    var1.c = 'z';  // overwrite it with the char again
```

```
        printdata();
        return 0;
}

void printdata()
{
    cout << "\nc = " << var1.c << ",\ti = " << var1.i << ",\tf = "
        << var1.f;
}
```

If you study this program's output, you can see that each time you change the value of one of the members, all the others are altered too, because at least one of the allocated bytes has been overwritten.

```
c = a,    i = 97,       f = 1.35926e-43
c = 2,    i = 50,       f = 7.006492e-44
c = R,    i = -18350,   f = 2.98
c = z,    i = -18310,   f = 2.98001
```

While unions allow a great deal of flexibility in dealing with data, the differences in size of each member can lead to inefficiency. In the example above, using variables of type DATA (which are four bytes long) to store single (one byte) characters would mean wasting three bytes in every four. However, unions can be ideal for handling cases where the type of data to be stored can vary depending on some external factor. Programmers sometimes use small unions nested inside larger structs to cope with this kind of situation.

5.6 Special uses

The **typedef** and **struct** keywords each have an additional, specialized use that you may encounter at some time or another.

In C (not C++) code, objects based on **enum**, **struct** or **union** types could not be declared in the same way as normal variables. Instead, the appropriate object keyword has to precede the name tag, like this:

```
// assume we have defined 'struct POINT'...

POINT Star;          // this is the new C++ way
struct POINT Moon;   // this is the older C way
```

To get around this inconvenience, C programmers use a **typedef** statement whenever a new enum, struct, or union is declared.

```
// two equivalent methods:
struct _POINT
{
    int x;
    int y;
};
typedef struct _POINT POINT;

// or:
typedef struct _POINT
{
    int x;
    int y;
} POINT;
```

Both of these coding styles can be found in the Standard Library header files, allowing structs and unions to be used in C code just as they would be in C++ code. In the example above, the **typedef** statement makes **POINT** a synonym for **struct _POINT**, so the statement **POINT Star;** works in both C and C++.

The second exception to normal use concerns the **struct** keyword. Most of the time, members of a structure are allocated memory according to their type. However, it is possible to create what is called a *bit field*, where members correspond directly to individual bits in a block of data. This technique is especially useful, for example, when dealing with a two-byte value whose individual bits are supposed to represent different items. Rather than performing several operations to extract the required information, the data is simply interpreted as a bit field structure and the members extracted effortlessly.

```
// define a structure with bit fields
struct CELL
{
    unsigned character : 8;     // 00000000 ????????
    unsigned foreground : 3;    // 00000??? 00000000
    unsigned intensity : 1;     // 0000?000 00000000
    unsigned background : 3;    // 0???0000 00000000
    unsigned blink : 1;         // ?0000000 00000000
};
```

This example uses the screen's normal text mode. In video memory, each character cell is represented by two bytes – the first holds the ASCII code of the displayed character, and the second controls the colour, intensity and blink flag. The structure **CELL** defined above neatly divides each of the bits of the two-byte pair into the appropriate group, thus saving the programmer the bother of extracting individual bits from the data. Notice that the members are not given a normal data type at all, because their size (in bits) is determined by the digit following their name.

The drawback to using bit field structures is that they depend on the programmer knowing the *order* that bytes are stored in memory. A program developed on an Intel CPU would have to be modified to run properly on a Motorola CPU, because the two systems actually store multi-byte values in a different order. Motorola chips are called *big-endian* because the largest byte is stored first, so a long integer (four bytes) with the value one would look like this in memory:

00 00 00 01

On the other hand, Intel chips are *little-endian* because the smallest byte is stored first. The same long integer would look like this:

01 00 00 00

For example, the struct **CELL** shown previously is written for Intel architecture. Although the member **CELL.character** occupies the *right-hand* byte, it actually appears *ahead* of the other byte in video memory. Fortunately, the compiler hides this kind of complication when you're dealing with normal variables.

5.7 Debugging your programs

Before you advance to the next chapter, it would help to understand how to use the debugging functions included with most compiler packages – being able to track down and fix programming errors quickly is a skill that develops with experience. If your code will not build correctly, it is always worth recompiling even before you have fixed all the reported errors – once the syntax rules are broken, the compiler can lose track of what can and can't come next, so one small typo can snowball into several reported errors. If the program compiles but it doesn't do what you expected, you can use your IDE's built-in debugger to track down the problem:

1 Set a *breakpoint* on the first line of code that you want to investigate (consult the on-line help for information on how to do this). A symbol or highlight usually appears over the line of code; when the program reaches this point, execution pauses and control is returned to the IDE.

2 You should now be able to *step* through the program one line at a time. Most compilers call this feature 'step over' or 'single step'; again, consult the on-line help for specific information. As each line is executed, you can keep track of variables by adding them to the *watch* window – choose **Add watch** from the **Debug** menu and type in the name of the object you want to track. A window should appear, displaying the value of the variable as you step through the code.

3 When you have finished testing, select **Run** to allow the program to complete execution in the normal way, or choose **Reset** or **Terminate** to kill the program and return immediately to the IDE for further editing.

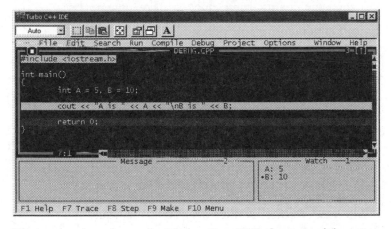

The screenshot shows the Turbo C++ IDE during a debugging session for a minimalist program. The first highlighted line shows the current position in the code; the second highlight represents a breakpoint. The watch window has been set to show the value of variables A and B, which have just been initialized.

Summary

The most significant part of this chapter was the introduction of functions and data scope. We looked at the declaration and the definition of a typical function, and learnt how data can be passed to and from functions as arguments and return values. A function is called by giving its name, followed by arguments of the correct or implicitly convertible types. Even a function that has no arguments must still have an empty set of parentheses. When the function returns, the resulting value can be stored in a variable or used in a more complex expression just like a simple constant would be.

You were introduced to the concept of scope – the lifetime and accessibility of a variable. Variables declared outside a function body are global; variables declared inside a function are local and are available only while the function is running. You can use the static type modifier to create local variables that are preserved between calls to a function. To access a global variable that is masked by a local one of the same name, you can use the scope resolution operator (::).

We looked at the more advanced ways of organizing data. Structures and unions allow several variables to be grouped into a single unit; you can use the member selection operator **.** to refer to each element. The **typedef** keyword is used to create shorthand names for specific variable types, and the **enum** keyword lets you assign meaningful names to a list of integers.

Finally, you were introduced to the concept of a debugger. Although the variation between compiler packages makes it impractical to give specific guidelines in this book, you should understand three central concepts – breakpoints, the watch window, and the single step command.

Exercises

1 Design a simple function that takes an integer argument
   and uses **cout** to display that number on the screen.
   Create a short demo program that calls the function a few
   times.

2 Expand the letter-categorizing program from Chapter 3
   so that the user can perform any number of tests before
   quitting. You will need to combine a loop structure with a
   function call.

3 Use functions and a global array of structures as necessary
   to create a program that gets user data for, say, three
   PERSON structures in turn and then prints the contents
   of each one.

06 the standard library: overview

In this chapter you will learn

- all about the Standard Library
- how to use it in your own code
- what standard functions are available

Aims of this chapter

This chapter explains how to access the library of pre-written functions that you can call from your program, and presents a selective overview of what is available. Look out for minor language elements that are introduced in the examples.

6.1 The C Standard Library

One of the things that separates C and C++ from other languages is the lack of any built-in keywords for performing input and output, basic mathematical calculations and utility tasks. Instead, every C and C++ compiler comes with a standard set of pre-written functions to handle these operations. It is called the C Standard Library, and as long as your compiler is compatible with the American National Standards Institute's original definition, which it almost certainly will be, the behaviour of these functions will be consistent with everybody else's. There are two main advantages to using a standard library:

- Because they are functions, just like the ones in your own source code, the calling method for performing a standard operation is exactly the same as the one for performing a function you have written yourself. This gives C and C++ more consistency than some other high-level languages.

- Because they must conform to an ANSI specification, you can be sure that the code you write for one compiler will work with another.

Compilers today provide their own extensions to the Standard Library, often including a large set of functions to make use of the computer's graphics capability. The unfortunate aspect of this development is that there is no standard governing these extensions, and the two main players – Borland and Microsoft – are not entirely consistent with one another. However, the rise in popularity of Microsoft Windows-based software has somewhat reduced this problem, because everything is accomplished through the standard Windows interface.

By this time you may be wondering exactly where all this standard code is kept. If you look at the directory of your compiler software, you will probably find two subdirectories called 'IN-CLUDE' and 'LIB' – or something similar. The INCLUDE directory contains a number of files containing the declarations needed by the compiler before the functions can be used in a program, and the actual code for the standard functions is spread across a number of library files (*.lib) in the LIB directory. This concept while become clearer as you read through the rest of this chapter.

6.2 Header files

The functions in the C Standard Library are very easy to use, with a little experience, and are indispensable to novice and expert programmers alike. To cover them all would be overkill, as you soon become familiar with the most important ones, so what follows is a selective overview of the library. Furthermore, the Standard Library is becoming less and less standard as compiler vendors compete to offer the most additional functionality, making it difficult to decide which functions can be regarded as commonplace and which as specific to certain packages. If you can't find a function listed here, search your compiler's on-line help; you will almost certainly find a similar function defined elsewhere. Functions that are not guaranteed to be standard are usually marked with an underscore before the name.

As you now know any variable or function must be declared before it can be used. Fortunately, all the necessary declarations for the Standard Library functions have already been prepared, and saved as text files in the INCLUDE directory of your compiler package. Although they are perfectly normal C/C++ source files, they are given the extension '.h' to indicate that they are *header* files – code that is usually inserted at the top (head) of your own source code file.

Although you could cut text out of these files and paste it directly into your source code, there is a neater way of accomplishing the same thing thanks to a part of the compiler known as the *preprocessor*. This runs before the main compilation, and it provides methods for making automatic textual changes to your source code before it is actually compiled. To automatically add all the necessary declarations for the C++ I/O functions to a source file takes only a single line:

```
#include <iostream.h>
```

This command, or preprocessor directive, means that the entire contents of the file **iostream.h** is automatically inserted into the source file at the point of the **#include** line, before the code is compiled. The <angle brackets> around the file name instruct the preprocessor to search the default directories for the **iostream.h** file. If "quotation marks" were used, the preprocessor would expect to find the file in the same directory as the current source file.

The declarations are spread across multiple header files so that you do not have to compile too many more lines than you need, but they also serve to group the library functions into common categories:

Include file	Description
assert.h	The assert macro, for debugging and testing
conio.h	Console (screen and keyboard) utility functions
ctype.h	Macros for determining character type (letter, digit, whitespace, etc.)
float.h	Advanced functions for floating-point arithmetic
fstream.h	Improved file handling functions, new to C++
io.h	Low-level file handling and utility functions
iostream.h	Improved input/output functions, new to C++
limits.h	Defines a number of platform-specific constants
malloc.h	Functions for dynamic memory allocation, now superseded
math.h	General mathematical functions
memory.h	Manipulation of memory blocks
search.h	Searching and sorting functions, also declared in **stdlib.h**
setjmp.h	Implementation of non-local jumps
stdarg.h	Allows use of variable length argument lists
stdio.h	Standard input/output routines for screen, files and memory
stdlib.h	Wide selection of common utility functions
string.h	Various functions for manipulation of strings
strstrea.h	Improved string handling functions, new to C++
time.h	System time and date handling

The files **fstream.h**, **iostream.h**, and **strstrea.h** are not strictly part of the original C library; they are part of the newer *streamed I/O* classes that belong to the C++ specification. Although they are designed to supersede much of the capability of the **stdio.h** functions, they do not prevent the use of the older system – in fact, both generations should work together without complication, although it is not recommended.

6.3 A brief tour of the library

As I have already emphasized, what follows is not an exhaustive reference to the standard library functions – you have the on-line help system for that. The aim here is simply to bring attention to what is available, so that you can continue your research as and when you need to. The next chapter looks at the application of particular functions in more detail.

assert.h

This include file defines a single macro, **assert**. Macros are covered in Chapter 8; for now, assume it is the same as a normal function. The assert macro is used during the debugging and testing phase to make sure (i.e. *assert*) that a condition or value is correct. For example:

```
#include <assert.h>
...
int main()
{
    // fetch a value from elsewhere
    int size = GetBlockSize();
    ...
    // if size is zero, there's a problem
    assert(size > 0);
    ...
}
```

If the expression passed to **assert** is false, execution of the program is stopped and an error message is printed. The exact message varies from compiler to compiler, but it usually takes the form '*Error in module.cpp, line 123: assertion failed*'.

It is important to realize that the **assert** macro is *only* for use during debugging, to test for errors in the flow of the program itself. In the code above, the possibility of **GetBlockSize** return-ing zero should already have been handled – the call to **assert** is actually testing that handling code by making sure that at this stage in the program flow, **size** is definitely non-zero. In other words, **assert** should be used to handle errors in your developing code, *not* errors due to external events at run-time.

Many compilers build two separate versions of the program ex-ecutable. The *debug* version contains extra data to allow step-by-step testing, and the *release* version is optimized for speed and size. In the release version, assert calls are automatically removed – another good reason not to use them for real error handling.

conio.h

This header file was not part of the original C library, but was introduced with Microsoft's Version Two Specification. Most modern compiler packages include this file. It defines a number of functions that add to the I/O facilities available through the **stdio.h** file. The difference is that these functions talk to the operating system for input and output, rather than using the hardware directly. Note that all these functions operate on the *console* – which is almost always the combination of the key-board, and the screen in standard text mode. However, the operating system can often be configured to take console com-mands from a different device, such as a remote terminal (the MS-DOS **ctty** command does this).

Function	Description
cputs/cgets	Console put string/console get string – simple in and out of strings
cprintf/cscanf	Console print formatted/console scan formatted – see stdio.h listing
getch/getche	Get character/get character with echo – gets the next keystroke
putch	Put character – write a single character to the console
ungetch	Undo get character – push a character back onto the input buffer
kbhit	Returns true if a keystroke is waiting in the buffer, false otherwise

ctype.h

The functions declared in this header all take a single character argument and return a Boolean (true or false) integer value. They are used to classify characters in routines that read and interpret strings.

Function	Returns true if character is...
isalnum	alphanumeric (A to Z, a to z, 0 to 9)
isalpha	alphabetic (A to Z, a to z)
isascii	valid ASCII (codes 0 to 127)
iscntrl	control character (codes 127 [Delete] and 0 to 31)
isdigit	numeric (0 to 9)
isgraph	graphical, i.e. visible (codes 33 to 126)
islower	lowercase (a to z)
isprint	printable (codes 32 to 126)
ispunct	punctuation (control characters or whitespace)
isspace	whitespace (space, tab, vertical tab, carriage return, new line, form feed)
isupper	uppercase (A to Z)
isxdigit	hexadecimal digit (0 to 9, A to F, a to f)

Most implementations also include two conversion functions, toupper and tolower, which are used to change the case of single characters and return the result.

```
/* ctypes.cpp (30/9/1999)
using ctype.h functions */

#include <ctype.h>
#include <iostream.h>

int main()
{
    char c;
    // prompt for a single character
    cout << "Enter a character";
    cin >> c;
```

```
// classify the character and print the result
if (isalpha(c))        cout << "\nAlphabetical";
else if (isdigit(c))   cout << "\nNumeric";
else if (ispunct(c))   cout << "\nPunctuation";
else                   cout << "\nUnclassified!";

    return 0;
}
```

float.h

The functions declared in this file are provided for dealing with very large or very accurate numbers, which are usually stored in variables of type double. Much of the functionality here conforms to the IEEE floating-point format standard; these routines are highly specialized and rely on good comprehension of the problems associated with representing non-real numbers on a computer. Rest assured; if you do not understand the meaning of these, you do not need to!

Function	Description
copysign (x, y)	Returns the value of x with the same sign as y
chgsign (x)	Returns the value of x, with the opposite sign
scalb(x, long y)	Scales x by a power of two – returns x * (2y)
logb(x)	Returns the exponential component of the value x
nextafter(x, y)	Returns the closest representable number to x in direction of y
finite(x)	Returns true is x is not infinite; false otherwise
isnan(x)	Returns true is x a 'NaN' (not a number); false otherwise
fpclass(x)	Returns the status word for floating-point class x

Note: all arguments are double, except for the **long** in **scalb**().

Float.h also defines a number of specific constants for use with these functions.

math.h

math.h declares a more general set of functions for everyday mathematical programming needs. Angles are always measured in radians. Although the basic group works with variables of type double, some implementations also include a group to work with floats (faster), and a group to work with long doubles (more accurate). These have the character **f** and **l** respectively, as a suffix to the normal function name. You may also find a set of mathematical constants are defined here; consult the documentation for specific information.

Function	Description
sin/asin/sinh	Sine/arcsine/hyperbolic sine of x
cos/acos/cosh	Cosine/arccosine/hyperbolic cosine of x
tan/atan/tanh	Tangent/arctangent/hyperbolic tangent of x
abs/fabs/labs	Absolute value of integer/float/long double x
floor	Rounds x down to nearest integer
ceil	Rounds x up to nearest integer
sqrt	Square Root ($\sqrt{x}$)
pow	Raise to power (x^y)
fmod	Floating-point remainder of x divided by y
log, log10	Return natural or base-10 logarithm of x
exp	e to the power of x ($e \approx 10^{2.71828}$)

Note: all arguments are in the form func(x) or func(x, y)

io.h

This header file declares functions for use with disk files. Be aware that although there is nothing wrong with the **open**, **read**, **write** and **close** functions listed here, most programs use the equivalent **fopen**, **fread**, **fwrite** and **fclose** functions from **stdio.h** because they are a little more flexible.

Function	Description
chmod	Sets or clears a file's read-only attribute
filelength	Returns the size of a named file

unlink Deletes files

rename	Renames files
open	Opens disk files (at low level)
read	Reads raw data from an open file
write	Writes raw data to an open file
close	Closes a file opened with the open function

limits.h

limits.h declares a number of constants for the minimum and maximum values that can be stored by the different primitive data types. This kind of information is useful when writing code that will be ported to several different platforms.

malloc.h

This file contains function that are used for dynamic memory allocation, but it became obsolete with the C++ **new** operator, which is described in Chapter 7.

setjmp.h

The functions **setjmp** and **longjmp** declared in this header file are used together to make jumps within your code. Unlike the **goto** keyword, this method is not restricted to the current source file but to *any* part of the code in the program – a powerful feature that can lead to 'spaghetti code' if used frequently. The **setjmp/longjmp** mechanisms are best used to deal with situations where an event, especially an error, needs to be handled quickly. However, many C++ implementations define a more efficient way to control errors, called *exception handling*.

stdarg.h

stdarg.h provides a way of writing functions that accept a variable number of arguments. This can be useful for handling variable-length lists of data items, as many of the functions in **stdio.h** do. One new data type and three macros are declared, and used together like this:

```
/* varargs.cpp (31/12/199)
variable arguments demo */

#include <iostream.h>
#include <stdarg.h>

// declare a function with variable number of args
float average(int count, ... );
// here's the definition
float average(int count, ... )
{
    float total;

    // initialize the system
    va_list va;
    va_start(va, count);

    // loop through extra the arguments
    for (int i = 1; i <= count; i++)         //inside declaration
        total += va_arg(va, float);

    // finish arg reading and return
    va_end(va);
    return (total / count);
}

// example calls
int main()
{
    float av1, av2;

    av1 = average(5, -1.0f, -4.0f, 6.0f, 0.0f, 10.0f);
    cout << "Average of -1, -4, 6, 0 and 10 is " << av1 << "\n";

    av2 = average(3, 134.66f, 0.18f, 28.11f);
    cout << "Average of 134.66, 0.18 and 28.11 is " << av2
<< "\n";

    return 0;
}
```

It's a reasonably simple system to get to grips with. First, a variable of type **va_list** is declared. Then, the **va_list** variable is passed in turn to **va_start()**, which also takes the last normal argument before the variable list as a reference marker – this means you must declare at least one normal argument in a function of this sort. Once this is done, as many calls to **va_arg**() can be made as there are variables in the list. When you are finished, call **va_end**() to reset the mechanism. The system relies on knowing how many bytes of data to pull off the calling stack for each argument (hence the keyword **float** appears in the call to **va_arg** in the example above), so for a function like this to work correctly, it is *very* important to use arguments of the right type. Since there is no way for the compiler to do any automatic conversion, the numerical constants that appear in the **main** function are all given the f suffix to make them floating-point. If you wanted to pass variables to this function, they would have to be cast first, by typing **float**(**variable**).

stdlib.h

This is the 'original' standard library header file, in that it contains a generous collection of useful functions for everyday programming tasks. The list varies between compilers; these are the most common ones:

Function	Description
abort	Aborts the program at the current point and prints a diagnostic message
atexit	Registers the functions to be called by the system before the program ends
exit	Ends the program at the current point, closing any open files first
getenv	Gets an environment string from the operating system
putenv	Adds a new environment string (equivalent to SET command in DOS)
searchenv	Searches for a file using the PATH environment string
system	Issues a user command to the operating system, such as 'dir'
rand	Returns a random integer between 0 and the constant RAND_MAX

srand	Seeds the random number generator with a new starting value
bsearch	Performs a binary search on an array of data (also found in search.h)
qsort	Re-orders an array of data using the quicksort algorithm. (also search.h)
ecvt/fcvt/gcvt	Converts a float to a string in various formatting methods
atoi/atof/atol	Converts a string of the form 123.456 to an integer / float / long double
itoa/ftoa/ltoa	Converts an integer / float / long double to a string
strod	String to double – reads a string and attempts conversion to a double
strtol	String to long – reads a string and attempts conversion to a long double
min	Macro that returns the smaller of two numbers
max	Macro that returns the larger of two numbers
fullpath	Converts file path from relative (..\file.txt) to absolute (c:\temp\file.txt)
makepath	Constructs a valid file path from drive, directory, name and extension
splitpath	Splits full paths into separate drive, directory, name and extension strings

Although most programs terminate by running to the end of the **main** function, you can use the **exit** function to quit from some other part of the code. **Exit** takes a single integer argument, which specifies the status code to quit with. This number translates to the MS-DOS *'errorlevel'* index and is equivalent to returning from **main** with an integer value. Most programs return zero if there were no fatal errors.

Environment variables, as maintained by the 'set' command on MS-DOS and Unix, can be accessed from a C++ program with the **getenv**, **putenv** and **searchenv** functions. You can use **getenv** and **setenv** to work with specific environment variables, while **searchenv** finds files within the directories specified by the 'path' variable. For more information on environment variables and the 'set' command, type 'set /?' or 'help set' at the DOS command prompt.

Random number generation is handled by the two **stdlib** functions **rand**, which returns random integers between 0 and the constant **RAND_MAX**, and **srand**, which sets the generator *seed*. It is actually impossible to generate a truly random number using a computer. Instead, the random number generator relies on a seed, or starting point, from which random integers are generated. If you initialize the generator with the same number every time, it will generate the same 'random' numbers!

The **fullpath**, **makepath** and **splitpath** functions can be indispensable for applications that must do a lot of file handling, and eliminate the need for several tedious calls to the normal string handling functions. You can use **fullpath** to convert a *relative* path, such as "..\readme.txt" to an *absolute* path, of the form "c:\programs\soundset\readme.txt". **makepath** and **splitpath** are used to convert between a full path name and its constituent parts, as in the example below:

```
#include <stdlib.h>

int main()
{
    // the constants _MAX_???? are defined in stdlib.h
    char fullpath[_MAX_PATH];
    char drive[_MAX_DRIVE];
    char directory[_MAX_DIR];
    char filename[_MAX_FNAME];
    char extension[_MAX_EXT];

    // create the pathname "c:\windows\system\kernel.dll"
    makepath(fullpath, "c", "\\windows\\system", "kernel", "dll");

    // now split it back into its parts
    splitpath(fullpath, drive, directory, filename, extension);

    return 0;
}
```

The **system** function provides a simple way of handling files or displaying directory information without actually writing any code:

```
#include <stdlib.h>
#include <iostream.h>

int main(void)
{
    // spawn the command interpreter
    cout << "About to run a DOS command...\n";
    system("dir");
    return 0;
}
```

memory.h

Memory.h declares three functions for handling memory blocks.

Function	Description
memcpy	Copies bytes from one memory address to another
memmove	Does the same as memcpy, but handles overlapping ranges correctly
memset	Sets a range of bytes to a certain value

These functions are also declared in **string.h** and are often used with strings. They take *pointers* – variables that contain memory addresses – as arguments, so the name of an array could be used here, because the bare name is a kind of pointer:

```
// set the first ten elements of int list[] to zero
// since integers take two bytes each, we must do 20 bytes
memset(list, 0, 20);
```

However, you can use the *referencing operator*, the ampersand **&**, to get the memory address of any variable that you want to use with a **memory.h** function. This technique is often used to zero-out a large structure without having to set each element individually:

```
// assume brother is an instance of struct PERSON
memset(&brother, 0, sizeof(brother));
```

The expression **&brother** returns the address of the start of the struct object **brother** in memory, and the expression **sizeof(brother)** returns its size in bytes.

Since **brother** is an instance of the **PERSON** struct, the expression **sizeof(PERSON)** had the same result and is interchangeable.

string.h

This file declares a comprehensive set of functions for working with strings, or more specifically, arrays of characters. They are all self-explanatory; for more detail on a specific function, refer to your compiler manual or on-line help.

Function	Description
strlen	Return the length of a string
strcmp	Compare two strings, case sensitive
strncmp	Compare first *n* letters of two strings, case sensitive
stricmp	Compare two strings, case insensitive
strnicmp	Compare first *n* letters of two strings, case insensitive
strcoll	Compare two strings using regional code page settings, case sensitive
stricoll	Compare first *n* letters of two strings using regional code page settings, case sensitive
strncoll	Compare two strings using regional code page settings, case insensitive
strnicoll	Compare first *n* letters of two strings using regional code page settings case insensitive
strlwr	Convert all letters of a string to lower case
strupr	Convert all letters of a string to upper case
strcpy	Copy one string to another
strncpy	Copy first *n* letters of one string to another
strcat	Append one string to another
strncat	Append first *n* letters of one string to another
strchr	Find the first occurrence of a certain character in a string
strrchr	Find the last occurrence of a certain character

in a string (the second 'r' is for "reverse")

strspn	Find first character in one string that is not present in another
strstr	Find first occurrence of one string in another
strtok	Search for tokens – substrings delimited by special characters – in a string
strdup	Duplicate a string (i.e. make a completely new copy in memory)
strrev	Reverse the characters in a string
strcspn	Find first character in one string that matches those in another
strset	Set all the characters in a string to a given value
strnset	Set the first *n* characters in a string to a given value
strpbrk	Find first character in one string that matches those in another
strxfrm	Convert a string based on current regional code page settings
strerror	Return a system- or user-defined error code

Of these, the **strcpy** function is probably the most used – since the assignment operator cannot be used with entire arrays, reinitializing a string takes this code:

```
strcpy(message, "Hello, World!\n");
```

time.h

All the time- and date-related functions you could ever wish for are declared in the **time.h** header file; many of them do almost exactly the same thing but with a different style of output.

The most important thing to remember is the way in which time is represented – at programming level, times and dates are usually given in seconds after 00:00:00 GMT on 1 January 1970. However, some implementations wrongly assume the system clock to be set to GMT regardless of the local time offset, which is supposed to be handled by the operating system. A little experimentation won't go amiss. Finally, be prepared to handle dates that run for a good many years into the future. Your program won't be around in 25 years' time? That's what they said in the 1970s, and look at Year 2000...

Summary

The Standard Library is an ever-growing collection of functions that help to simplify everyday programming tasks. Declarations of functions, global variables and constants are grouped into a number of header files, which are added to the top of a C++ program using the **#include** directive. When you build the program, the linker retrieves the required code from library files in the compiler's LIB directory.

You have seen the huge range of functions and some examples of their use. Two specific coding techniques were explicitly introduced:

◆ You can zero-out a whole structure with a single line of code: **memset(&mystruct, 0, sizeof(mystruct));** – this saves accessing each member in turn. The use of the **&** symbol is fully explained in Appendix B.

◆ Since the assignment operator doesn't work on arrays, the code to store a literal string into a character array is **strcpy(chararray, "literal string");**.

Exercises

1 Get a string from the user and print it back in its original form, then in uppercase, in lowercase, and finally backwards. Use **string.h** to help you.

2 Write a program that displays a neat string containing the date and time, in both GMT and local zone formats.

3 Create a utility that gets the name of a file from the user and outputs the size of the file. You will need to use the **open** and **close** functions to manipulate the file handle.

07

the standard library: techniques

In this chapter you will learn

- how to control the formatting of your input and output
- how to read and write files on disk
- how to use command-line arguments with your program
- how to allocate memory space on-the-fly

Aims of this chapter

This chapter describes a number of techniques that can significantly enhance the functionality of your programs. First, we will look at the formatted I/O and file handling capability provided by the stdio.h header file. You'll also learn how to read program arguments from the command line, and be introduced to dynamic memory allocation, the mechanism used to create and delete storage space on-the-fly.

7.1 Classic C I/O

Stdio.h contains a treasure-trove of I/O functions that have been with the C and C++ languages ever since their creation. Although version two of the C++ specification introduced **iostream.h**, **strstrea.h** and **fstream.h**, which are meant to re-place and improve on the original **stdio.h** capability, so many programs and programmers still use the old style that it is well worth learning about them. Indeed, there are numerous situa-tions where the sheer flexibility of these functions makes them much more useful than their newer counterparts. However, you were introduced to the more modern **cout** method at first be-cause it does more of the work for you.

printf

The **printf** function – the 'f' is for *formatted* – handles all kinds of general-purpose output, writing the resultant text to the specially-defined object *stdout*, which is almost always mapped to the computer screen. The **cout << [data]** statement that you have been using already is equivalent to this. Data is passed to the function using a two-part system. The first argument to **printf** is always a *format string*, which contains plain text and any number of extra *format specifiers*. The second part is a vari-able-length argument list which passes the data for each specifier.

A format specifier is marked by the percent sign % and con-tains optional and required fields. The **printf** function uses the information to decide how a string of bytes in a variable should be represented by digits and separators on the screen; since every value is represented by the same old 1s and 0s in memory, it is important to specify how it should be interpreted. The syntax for a format specifier is as follows:

printf() format specifier syntax:

%[flags][width][.precision][size]type

flags	Leading zeros, justification mode, etc.
width	Minimum number of characters to fill
precision	Maximum number of characters to fill
size	Modifies the size of the 'type' field
type	Required specification of data type

Common types are:

%c	Single character
%s	String (character array)
%d or %i	Signed decimal integer
%o	Signed octal integer
%u	Unsigned decimal integer
%f	Floating point, [xxxx].[yyyy]
%x or %X	Hexadecimal, with a–f or A–F
%e or %E	Floating point, [x].[yyy]e[zz]
%g or %G	Either %f or %e depending on size

See Appendix C for flags, width, precision, and size options

Often, all you will need to specify is the type field, which is required for every format specifier. However, it is worth being aware of the options provided by the other four fields, which together give the programmer a great deal of power. The listing below demonstrates **printf**, just using the 'type' part of the format specifier:

```
/* printf.cpp (30/9/1999)
demo of printf function */

#include <stdio.h>
int main()
```

```
{
    // set data to some arbitrary value
    int data = -12345;

    // print all the different interpretations of those two bytes
    printf("Representation of the 2 bytes in the integer data:");
    printf("\nSigned Decimal Integer: %d", data);
    printf("\nSigned Octal (base 8) Integer: %o", data);
    printf("\nUnsigned Decimal Integer: %u", data);
    printf("\nUnsigned Hexadecimal (base 16) Integer: %x or
        %X", data, data);
    printf("\nFloating Point Number: %f", (float)data);
    printf("\nFloating Point in Exponential Format: %e",
        (float)data);
    return 0;
}
```

You may be surprised to see how many ways there are to interpret those two bytes:

```
Representation of the 2 bytes in the integer data:
Signed Decimal Integer: -12345
Signed Octal (base 8) Integer: 147707
Unsigned Decimal Integer: 53191
Unsigned Hexadecimal (base 16) Integer: cfc7 or CFC7
Floating Point Number: -12345.000000
Floating Point in Exponential Format: -1.234500e+04
```

It is important to remember that the variable **data** represents
the same sixteen bits of data every time – by changing the type
flag passed to **printf**, you alter the *interpretation* of the information. This behaviour contrasts with the **cout << [data]**
method, which decides on the interpretation for you, by looking at the variable type. The fact that the programmer tells
printf how to represent the data makes it extremely powerful.
Notice how the character representation of the variable passed
to **printf** is inserted into the format string at the position marked
by the format specifier. If there are no format specifiers, no
more arguments need to be passed – as in the very first call to
printf shown above.

scanf

The sister function to **printf** is **scanf**. While **printf** converts raw data into formatted text, **scanf** converts formatted text into raw numerical data. The syntax is similar to that for **printf**, with a formatting string followed by a variable-length argument list. However, you must remember always to pass the address of the target variables, not the variables themselves. To do this, you use the referencing operator, **&**.

```
/* scanf.cpp (30/9/1999)
demo of scanf function */

#include <stdio.h>

int main()
{
    float fraction; int uint;

    // get some numbers and print them back out
    printf("\nPlease enter an unsigned integer: ");
    scanf("%u", &uint);

    printf("\nPlease enter a fraction: ");
    scanf("%f", &fraction);

    printf("\n\nYou entered %u and %.2f", uint, fraction);
    return 0;
}
```

Output:

```
Please enter an unsigned integer: 3
Please enter a fraction: 0.51234
You entered 3 and 0.51
```

The **scanf** function gets a string typed at the keyboard and then attempts to convert it into the numerical format given by the format string, which usually contains just a single format specifier. The process stops as soon as the function gets to a character that cannot be interpreted in the context of the current conversion, so if you enter "abc" when asked for an integer, **scanf** will fail immediately. You can check for errors by looking at the integer value returned by **scanf**, as this contains the number of fields successfully converted (in the example above, this value should be 1 both times). Notice here how the output of fraction is limited to two decimal places by the .2 in the second format specifier.

7.2 Simple file handling

Creating, reading and writing files couldn't be easier with the Standard Library. In fact, formatted input and output is performed in exactly the same style as before – but instead of **printf** and **scanf**, you now use **fprintf** and **fscanf**. You can also read and write bytes directly between variables and files using the functions **fread** and **fwrite**. To use any of these functions however, you must pass a special pointer which identifies the target file and controls all access to it. This pointer is known as a file handle, and is returned by the most important function of the group, **fopen**. Files must be opened by **fopen** before any other action can be performed on them, and closed afterwards with **fclose**. A small demonstration should make everything clear:

```
/* files.cpp (30/9/1999)
file handling with stdio.h */

#include <stdio.h>

int main()
{
    char agent[] = "Bond";
    FILE* textfile = NULL;

    // use fopen() to create a file, then check for errors
    textfile = fopen("demo.txt", "w");
    if (!textfile) return -1;

    // OK: write it, close it, and quit
    fprintf(textfile, "The name is %s. James %s.", agent,
        agent);
    fclose(textfile);
    return 0;
}
```

There are a number of things to look at:

- The variable textfile is actually a pointer (see Chapter 9) to the **FILE** structure declared in **stdio.h**, and is initialized with the value NULL. Although NULL is actually just a macro for the integer zero, it is used to make it obvious to anyone reading the code that this number is a pointer of zero, not just a zero value.

- The **fopen** function tries to return a handle to the file 'demo.txt'. The second argument, "**w**", specifies what specific action to take – the full range of options is tabulated below. If textfile is still zero after the call to fopen, the operation must have failed, so the **main** function returns early.

- A simple string is written to the file. Notice how **fprintf** is used in almost exactly the same way as **printf**; the only difference is the extra argument at the beginning which specifies a valid file handle to write to. Additional calls to **fprintf** or **fwrite** would place data immediately after the current string.

- Finally, the file is closed with the **fclose** function. This means that **textfile** is no longer valid, even though it still points somewhere in memory. If the program isn't just about to exit, it is always a good idea to reassign **NULL** to unused file handles so that unintentional misuse does not corrupt memory.

- If everything went according to plan, a new file 'demo.txt' will have been created in the current directory, containing the sentence "The name is Bond. James Bond." This file will be overwritten each time you run the program.

To read from a file, you can use **fscanf** in the same way as you would normally use **scanf**, except that the first argument is now the file handle. However, for the call to be successful you must be sure to open the file in a mode that allows reading. In the previous example, a call to **fscanf** would fail because the file was opened in write-only mode. There are four important modes to remember:

Mode Description

"r"   Open an existing file for reading only.

"w"   Create a file for writing only. Existing copies are overwritten.

"r+"   Open an existing file for both reading and writing.

"w+"   Open a file for both reading and writing. Existing copies are overwritten.

The "w" and "w+" modes should be used with care – the very act of opening an existing file in these modes will destroy all the data contained therein. You may also want to specify whether to interpret the file as raw binary data or text, by adding a "b" or a "t" to the end of the mode string. In text mode, the carriage-return/linefeed pair used to signal a new line is automatically converted to a single linefeed character on input, and vice versa on output. If no extra character is specified, **fopen** defaults to the mode specified in the system-level global variable **_fmode**.

7.3 Blocked I/O

Here's a program that dumps the contents of a text file to the console. Be sure to change **FILENAME** to the name of a suitable file in the same directory as textdump.exe or the program will exit early.

```
/* textdump.cpp (30/9/1999)
blocked I/O demo */

#include <stdio.h>
#define FILENAME "arith.cpp"
#define BUFFER_LENGTH 1024

int main()
{
    // create a large buffer to store the data
    char block[BUFFER_LENGTH + 1];

    // a normal integer, and a special file handle
    int bytesread;
    FILE* handle = NULL;

    // try to open the file and check for success
```

```
        handle = fopen(FILENAME, "r");
        if (!handle) return -1;

        do {
            // read a block of data from the file
            bytesread = fread(block, 1, BUFFER_LENGTH, handle);

            // add a terminating null so it becomes a legal string
            block[bytesread] = '\0';

            // print the block
            printf(block);

        // loop if we got as many bytes as we asked for
        } while (bytesread == BUFFER_LENGTH);

        // close the file and quit
        fclose(handle);
        return 0;
    }
```

The code has fairly advanced structure because it uses *blocked I/O*. Instead of reading from the disk file one byte at a time, the function loads entire *blocks* into memory for processing. This is a far more efficient method because, due to the architecture of the hard disk and the filing system, reading a few kilobytes takes only a fraction longer than reading one byte. The disadvantage is that dealing with blocks can be slightly more complicated than dealing with single bytes. The trick is to repeatedly compare the number of bytes successfully read with the number requested, so that you can tell when the end of the file has been reached.

The outer **do...while** loop works through each new block in turn. Within the loop body, the first statement is a call to **fread**, which tries to read **BUFFER_LENGTH** bytes from the file handle **handle** into the array **block**. The number of bytes *actually* read is returned by **fread** and stored in the variable **bytesread**. If **bytesread** is not equal to **BUFFER_LENGTH**, the **fread** function must have encountered an error or the end of the file, so the loop ends.

Each block, whether it is complete or incomplete, is processed by the two statements that appear after the call to **fread**. Since

bytesread holds the number of valid bytes in the buffer, **block[bytesread]** is the first of the unused bytes, so we set this to zero so that **block** becomes a normal null-terminated string. The character constant '\0' is used for clarity, although a plain 0 would work perfectly well. The buffer is then written to the screen with a simple call to **printf**.

7.4 Trick string manipulation

While it may not seem like a true form of output, **stdio.h** also includes a pair of functions for reading from and writing to character arrays in memory. You can use the **sprintf** and **sscanf** functions exactly as you do their original counterparts, except that the first argument is now the name of the string. For example:

```
char result[100];
char s1[] = "Giraffe";
char s2[] = "Elephant";
int i1 = -200;
unsigned int u1 = 123;
float f1 = 1.234;

// a very easy way to cobble all those together!
sprintf(result, "%s\n%s\n%i, %u, %f", s1, s2, i1, u1, f1);
```

If you want make some kind of textual output using a function that only accepts strings, **sprintf()** provides a very easy way to perform all the necessary conversion of substrings, integers, and floats into a final array of characters that you can pass on to another function. In this example, the string **result** now reads:

```
Giraffe
Elephant
-200, 123, 1.234000
```

In summary, the **printf** and **scanf** families provide a simple way of converting between human-readable text and machine-readable data. Both families use format specifiers – special symbols, prefixed with a percent sign, that contain information about the desired representation of data. The **fprintf** and **fscanf** functions work in the same way as **printf** and **scanf** but are supported by **fopen** and **fclose**, which control actual access to files, and **fread** and **fwrite,** which are used to write larger blocks of raw data. Similarly, **sprintf** and **sscanf** provide the same formatted I/O for strings in memory.

7.5 The C++ alternative: iostream.h

iostream.h and its partners **fstream.h** and **strsrtea.h** were introduced with C++ and were designed to replace the functionality provided by the older **stdio.h** header. They are easy to use, especially for simple operations, but they rely on several advanced topics that are not covered until Chapter 10. For this reason, I will continue to use **cout** and **cin** as before, but will not attempt to explain how to format the output, or handle files and strings, until later. In the meantime, I recommend that you use the **printf** and **scanf** family whenever you need more control – many professional programmers still do.

7.6 Reading program arguments

For any program that is started from the command line, you can add extra options (*command line arguments*) to control what the program does or which file it should act on. To access the arguments that were passed to your program, you need to declare the **main** function differently:

```
/* printarg.cpp (30/9/1999)
demo of argc and argv */

#include <stdio.h>

// define main with two special arguments
// these values are set by the operating system

int main(int argc, char *argv[])
{
    // iterate through each argument
    for (int i = 0; i < argc; i++)
    {
        // print the index number and the corresponding string
        printf("%u\t%s\n", i, argv[i]);
    }
    return 0;
}
```

The first argument, **argc**, is simply the number of arguments on the command line. Most operating systems send the name of the program file itself as the first argument, so **argc** is always greater than or equal to one. The second argument is an array of pointers to characters, or alternatively, a pointer-to-pointer-to-char – you'll understand the significance once you've read Chapter 9. For now, all you need to know is that **argv[n]** returns the *n*th command line argument. Try running the program above with a command like:

    C:\TC\BIN>printarg this is a test

The output should read:

    0   C:\TC\BIN\PRINTARG.EXE
    1   this
    2   is
    3   a
    4   test

The **for** loop iterates through each argument, printing the number i and the corresponding string **argv[i]** each time.

7.7 Dynamic memory allocation

So far, you have allocated memory by declaring all the variables you will need at the beginning of a program. This system is perfectly adequate in most situations, but it does force the programmer to decide exactly how much storage is needed *before* the program is run; in some cases, this is simply not possible. Instead, you can allocate and de-allocate memory whenever you need it using the **new** and **delete** operators.

You may prefer to read Chapter 9 before continuing this section – since the DMA mechanism deals with the memory subsystem at a fairly low level, it makes extensive use of *pointers*, which are variables designed to hold the *address* of other objects in memory:

new operator syntax:

    pType = new type;

type   any C++ variable or object type
pType a pointer to the same type

The **new** operator tries to allocate enough memory from the *heap* (the global free memory store maintained by the system) to create a new variable of the specified type. If it succeeds, it returns a pointer to this new object; if it fails, it returns zero.

```
/* new.cpp (30/9/1999)
using the DMA keywords */

#include <stdio.h>

int main()
{
    // declare a pointer to an integer
    int* pInteger;

    // allocate two bytes from the heap,
    // storing the address of the new space in pInteger
    pInteger = new int;
    if (!pInteger) return -1;

    // assign a value and then print the data
    *pInteger = 10;
    printf("pInteger = %p, Contents = %i", pInteger, *pInteger);

    // deallocate again
    delete pInteger;
    return 0;
}
```

The output is just another one-liner:

```
pInteger = 059A, Contents = 10
```

Here, we are using the **new** operator to dynamically allocate an integer variable; since it only takes two bytes there is a very good chance that the system will succeed. However, you should always check the value of the pointer variable after an allocation attempt – if it *is* null, you may crash the system when you try to write to it. In this example, the program returns immediately if the **new** operator returns zero.

Once they have been allocated, heap objects can be used in exactly the same way as normal variables, as the middle two lines of code demonstrate. Exactly the same? The one important distinction is that any object created from the heap exists until the program ends or until it is explicitly destroyed. Scope rules do not apply here; even if you lose the original pointer, the heap memory itself still remains bound to the program. To avoid an eventual out-of-memory error, you should always use the **delete** operator to deallocate heap objects as soon as you have finished using them:

delete operator syntax:

> delete pointer;

or

> delete[] array;

pointer   pointer to previously allocated variable

array   pointer to (i.e. name of) previously allocated array

Although the heap is cleaned up automatically at the end of the program, the example above explicitly destroys the integer pointed to by **pInteger** before returning. Note the square brackets in the second form of **delete** syntax – if you were to allocate an array and then destroy it *without* the square brackets, the system would only deallocate the first array element.

```
// allocate 1024 bytes
char* pBuffer - new char[1024];

// bug: this deallocates only the first byte
delete pBuffer;

// correct: this deallocates all 1024 bytes
delete[] pBuffer;
```

Summary

This chapter introduced some of the more advanced capabilities of the standard library. You now have far more control over the formatting of screen output thanks to the **printf** function. We saw how to manipulate strings quickly and easily using **sprintf** and **sscanf**, and practised simple file handling with **fprintf** and **fscanf**.

Blocked I/O involves using a large buffer for reading data from file into memory. Although this technique is more efficient, it can complicate the code – the example we looked at shows how to handle this situation. You were also introduced to the extra arguments to the main function that you can use to retrieve command-line parameters.

Finally, you saw how to dynamically allocate memory using the **new** operator, and de-allocate it using the **delete** operator. This feature makes it easy to handle data objects that need to expand or shrink during the course of a program.

Exercises

1 Modify **textdump.cpp** so that the filename can be specified on the command line by the user. Try adding support for more than one file at a time.

2 Create a program that 'encrypts' a file by reversing its contents and saving it back to disk. You should be able to recover the original file by running the program a second time. Allocate buffer memory dynamically.

08

the preprocessor

In this chapter you will learn

- how to use macros to speed up code-writing
- how to create conditional compilation structures
- how to change compiler settings and options within your code

Aims of this chapter

This chapter introduces the preprocessor, a mechanism for handling certain *directives* that perform automatic additions and modifications to your code before it is actually compiled. We will discuss the **#include** directive, which you have already been using, as well as **#define**, which is used to create word processor-like text macros, and the **#if...#else...#endif** directives.

8.1 The preprocessor

The preprocessor is actually just another part of the compiler, but it works almost completely separately from the actual code compilation. The directives are not a part of the C++ language, but are a text-based system of shortcuts that save repetitive typing and cumbersome source files. Before it is compiled, source code is preprocessed – text is added or removed, and macros are expanded. This results in a 'clean' source file, containing only pure C++, which is then compiled. Directives are distinguished from normal code by a preceding hash (#) sign. Note also that semicolons are not required; the end of the line signifies the end of the directive. To continue a directive across multiple lines, put a backslash at the end of all but the last line.

8.2 The #include directive

As you have already been using it, I will start with **#include**:

#include directive syntax:

    #include <filename>

or

    #include "filename"

The purpose of **#include** is simply to include the entire contents of the file given by "filename" in the current file, starting on the line with the **#include** directive itself. Although it is generally used for header files, you could use this directive to add the contents of any other text file to your source code. Of course, it would have to be syntactically correct C or C++ code if you actually wanted it to compile.

The difference between the two styles relates simply to the locations searched by the preprocessor for the named file. Names separated by <angle brackets> will be searched for in the default locations (usually a subdirectory of the compiler package called INCLUDE), while names separated by quotation marks will first be searched for in the directory of the current source file, before the default locations are checked.

8.3 The #define and #undef directives

Rather like the macro and auto-correction facilities in a word processor, the preprocessor provides a way of defining meanings for simple identifiers. During the preprocessing phase, each identifier is replaced with its actual meaning. This is useful in itself, but the mechanism goes one step further and allows function-like shortcuts, or *macros*, to be defined as well. All this is achieved through the #define directive:

#define directive syntax:

    #define NAME

or

    #define NAME meaning

or

    #define NAME(arguments, ...) meaning

Unlike **#include**, the three different forms of **#define** have sufficient variation to discuss them separately. However, one thing that all three have in common is a unique name, which is the label by which any definition or macro is referenced. Since the preprocessing phase always replaces this name identifier with something else, it does not have to conform to C++ syntax rules, but it must not contain any spaces. It is convention to make all **#define**d names upper case, to distinguish them from function and variable names.

The command to undefine a previously defined identifier is the same whichever form of **#define** was used. Just use the **#undef** directive with the name of the identifier:

#undef directive syntax:

    #undef NAME

NAME must have been previously defined by **#define**.

It may surprise you that after all this discussion of replacement, the first and simplest form of **#define** involves no replacement! All that matters in this form is that the identifier has been defined. This is not for replacement purposes, but is instead for the benefit of the next set of commands – the conditional compilation directives, which are covered later in this chapter.

The second form of **#define** directive is probably the most used, and is also simple to understand. During the preprocessing phase, every instance of **NAME** is replaced with the string defined for it. This feature is especially useful for assigning meaningful strings to values, so that rather than code that reads:

    SetBrush(0, 3, 1);   // meaning of values not clear

...the programmer can use:

    SetBrush(COLOUR_BLACK, SIZE_LARGE, STYLE_DOTS);

Of course, this relies on those three identifiers being defined first. Such information would probably be put in a header file along with the declaration of the **SetBrush** function, out of the way of the main code:

    #define COLOUR_BLACK 0
    #define COLOUR_BLUE 1
    ...
    #define SIZE_LARGE 3
    ...
    #define STYLE_DOTS 1
    #define STYLE_SOLID 0
    ...

The great thing about this method of value-labelling is that to the compiler the two ways of calling **SetBrush** are identical – no extra code is generated because the preprocessor has already converted the identifiers back into the correct numbers before compilation begins for real.

The same method is useful for defining values and strings that are constant throughout the execution of the program. Defining a name for these values means that should you want to change one of them, you need only change the definition, and not every single instance of it. This saves time and reduces the potential for mistakes. For example:

```
/* define.cpp (30/9/1999)
using #define directives */

#include <stdio.h>
#define VERSION_STRING "Version 1.0, 28th August 1999"

int main()
{
    // print welcome message
    printf("Artificial Intelligence %s\n", VERSION_STRING);

    // to do: add artificial intelligence code ...

    // print closing message and quit
    printf("Thanks for using AI %s!", VERSION_STRING);
    return 0;
}
```

The output is proof that the substitution works:

```
Artificial Intelligence Version 1.0, 28th August 1999
Thanks for using AI Version 1.0, 28th August 1999!
```

On to the third form. Although a little more complex than labelling values, defining a few good macros early on in a large project can save a lot of time later on. To recap, the general syntax is:

```
#define NAME(arguments, ...) meaning
```

As before, the name identifier is replaced by its more complex meaning, but in this more sophisticated version, any number of further arguments can be specified. These new arguments are then transplanted as values into the replacement string. A few examples should help:

```
// define a macro that gives the product of two numbers –
#define PRODUCT(x, y) ((x)*(y))
```

Here, the preprocessor converts the code **PRODUCT(10, 20)** into **((10)*(20))**, and **PRODUCT(abc, def)** into ((abc)*(def)). This is obviously a completely pointless macro, because it is far easier to just type $x*y$ than **PRODUCT(x, y)**. However, it demonstrates the syntax – notice how each argument finds its way into the replacement string. Since the preprocessor is fundamentally crude, there is absolutely no syntax or type checking, and the arguments are blindly transplanted into the resulting string. Now for a slightly more useful macro:

```
// macro that gives the mid-point of two x,y points - the
// backslash continues the definition onto the next line.
#define MIDPOINT(x1, y1, x2, y2) \
((((x1)+(x2))/2),(((y1)+(y2))/2))
```

Thus, **MIDPOINT(10, 10, 20, 20)** becomes $((((10)+(20))/2),(((10)+(20))/2))$ which will be compiled as $(15,15)$. The enclosing parentheses are always a good idea, to avoid misinterpretation within compound expressions.

This time, **MIDPOINT(10, 10, 20, 20)** is certainly much clearer than its expanded equivalent. This example also demonstrates how easily macro definitions can become extremely complicated, due to the fact that any calculations or conversions have to be done in a single giant step, rather than being broken down into several normal C++ statements. Even this simple macro requires several layers of parentheses to get the right result. Because of this, always make sure that it is worth using a macro to complete a given task – beyond simple conversions and text-based tricks, it is probably better to use a proper function, which will also carry the benefits of the compiler's type and syntax checking. You should also remember that a macro is reinserted and later recompiled afresh every time its main identifier appears in the source code. Functions, on the other hand, are compiled only once, which means that only one copy of the procedure ends up in the final executable file.

8.4 Macro traps

The main benefit of using macros is faster execution, because the small overhead of calling and returning from a function is eliminated. However, macro side-effects may mean that arguments are treated incorrectly when anything more complicated than a simple value is passed.

You may have noticed that the two example macros **PRODUCT** and **MIDPOINT** both place brackets directly around their arguments – this prevents the first side-effect, incorrect order of evaluation. Consider for a moment a version of the

PRODUCT macro without the extra brackets:

```
#define PRODUCT(x, y) (x*y)
```

This macro works fine when called with simple values, but if either argument is itself an expression, problems arise. If we called the macro like this:

```
int result, width = 120, height = 110;
result = PRODUCT(width + 20, height - 10);
```

…since **width+20** is 140 and **height-10** is 100, we might expect the macro to evaluate to 14,000. It doesn't. To find out why, it helps to work out exactly how the preprocessor expands the macro before it is passed to the compiler:

```
PRODUCT(width + 20, height - 10)
```

is expanded by the preprocessor to

```
(width + 20*height - 10)
```

which, since multiplication takes precedence over addition, is equivalent to

```
(width + (20 * height) - 10)
```

Thus, the **PRODUCT** macro unexpectedly returns 2310. To avoid this problem, the arguments x and y are enclosed in their own brackets in the macro definition. The expansion then becomes

```
((width + 20)*(height - 10))
```

which ensures that the macro works the way you expect it to.

You'll encounter the second trap when a macro evaluates its arguments more than once. For instance, the macro below returns the absolute value of its argument (i.e. negative sign removed), and is more powerful than a function because it works with any numerical data type.

```
#define absolute(x) (((x) < 0) ? –(x) : (x))
```

However, the macro has an undesirable side-effect when called like this:

```
a = absolute(a++);
```

The line above expands to

```
a = (((a++) < 0) ? –(a++) : (a++));
```

The example code increments **a** when passing it to **absolute**, but the expanded macro evaluates the argument **a++** twice, once to check the sign, and again for the result, therefore increasing **a** by two, not one. This problem is difficult to cure efficiently; in most cases it's better to simply avoid the issue by incrementing **a** in a separate statement.

8.5 Conditional compilation

On top of the functionality provided by **#include** and **#define**, the preprocessor command set includes a comprehensive set of directives that allow conditional compilation – a mechanism for controlling which parts of the code are compiled under certain conditions. Most of them have similar relatives in the C++ language itself, so their meaning is usually obvious. Here is a quick list:

Directive	Description
#if expression	If expression is non-zero, lines below this are compiled
#ifdef NAME	If NAME is defined, lines below this are compiled
#ifndef NAME	If NAME is not defined, lines below this are compiled
#else	#else is to #if as the C++ 'else' is to the C++ 'if'
#elif expression	Equivalent to "#else #if expression"
#endif	Marks the end of an #if, #ifdef or #ifndef block

There are actually two ways of achieving the same thing with this set of directives, because you can use either the **#if...#elif...#else...#endif** style or the **#ifdef...#else...#endif** and **#ifndef...#else...#endif** styles.

The former style is more flexible if you have a complicated system of conditions to implement, but the latter pair is slightly simpler and is usually sufficient for the task. Incidentally, the operator **defined** can be used with the **#if** and **#elif** directives. Thus **#if defined(NOCHECKS)** is exactly the same as **#ifdef NOCHECKS**.

A common use of this mechanism can be found in header files – look in any of the Standard Library headers and you will see all manner of conditional compilation tricks. To prevent a header from being accidentally included more than once, for example, the entire file can be surrounded by an **#ifndef** block:

```
#ifndef __STDIO_H
#define __STDIO_H
…
#endif
```

When the file is first processed, the code inside the **#ifndef** block is compiled because the constant __STDIO_H has not yet been defined. However, a #**define** directive somewhere in that block *does* define __STDIO_H, which prevents subsequent recompilation. The same sort of system can be used to compile different lines of code depending on the current platform and its requirements. To help with this, the compiler system usually defines a number of global identifiers and macros that can be used to check on the current environment. Their exact names differ between compiler version and manufacturer, but you can be fairly sure of the following:

Identifier	Defined as
__DATE__	String containing the date that processing began on this file
__TIME__	String containing the time that processing began on this file
__FILE__	String containing the file name of the current source file
__LINE__	Number of the source file line being processed
__STDC__	Constant equal to one if only standard C keywords are being used
__cplusplus	Defined if the compiler is in C++ mode, otherwise undefined
__PASCAL	Defined if Pascal calling mode is set, otherwise undefined

These can be useful for controlling exactly how your code is compiled:

```
#ifndef __cplusplus
#error Sorry, C++ required!
#endif

#include <iostream.h>

int main()
{
    cout << "Compiled at " << __TIME__ << " on " <<
        __DATE__;
    cout << "\nThis is line " << __LINE__ << " of " <<
        __FILE__;
    return 0;
}
```

The **#error** directive used here simply outputs error messages to the compiler's standard message window. If __**cplusplus** is defined there will be no fatal error message and the main code will be compiled.

The same process works in reverse – as well as getting information on compiler settings from pre-defined identifiers, you can also *set* certain elements of compiler behaviour by defining special constants in your source code. The most common of these is **NDEBUG** ('no debugging') which turns off certain aspects of code generation used for debugging. If you add **#define NDEBUG** before **#include <assert.h>**, the **assert** macro is automatically commented out. This means that you can quickly remove extra testing code that was used during development before compiling the final version of your program. Try this code, then uncomment the first line, recompile and re-run.

```
//#define NDEBUG

#include <assert.h>
#include <stdio.h>
int main()
{
    // this should fail
    assert(0);

    printf("Terminating Normally.");
    return 0;
}
```

8.6 The #pragma directive

The last directive worth discussing is **#pragma**. You will find it implemented in many different compilers for many different languages, but once again, consistency is practically non-existent. Generally, **#pragma** allows compiler options and settings to be written directly into the source file that requires them. For example, most C++ compilers support a **#pragma startup function_name** directive which can be used to register functions that need to be called before the **main** function, and a **#pragma exit function_name** directive for registering functions that must be called before the program exits. To get a full list of the **#pragma** directives available with your compiler package, consult the user guide or on-line help and search the index for **#pragma**.

Summary

The preprocessor can provide a neat way of solving many programming problems. You can seamlessly add other source files to your code using the **#include** directive, and define constants or function-like macros using the **#define** directive. Macros are generally faster than functions but they take up more space because they are reinserted and recompiled each time they are called. They have no type checking, and careless use can cause unforeseen problems as in the **absolute(a++)** example outlined earlier. However, they do provide a quick and easy way of automating certain operations.

The **#if**, **#ifdef** and **#ifndef** directives provide a mechanism for conditional compilation, which controls which lines of code are actually sent to the compiler depending on certain critical conditions. This system is useful for handling cross-platform differences or for ensuring that the correct compilation environment is used. The predefined identifiers listed above can help with this, as can the **#pragma** directive, which configures several compiler options.

Exercises

1 Look up **#pragma** in the on-line help and find what options your compiler has.

2 Open up **assert.h** and prove to yourself that defining **NDEBUG** disables the **assert** macro. Look out for other uses of conditional compilation in the file.

3 Write a program that outputs a neatly formatted list of all the pre-defined variables (**__DATE__**, **__FILE__**, etc.) that your compiler supports.

09

advanced topics

In this chapter you will learn

- how to access memory directly using pointers
- how to write more efficient functions using pass-by-reference
- how to use variables and functions declared in external source files

Aims of this chapter

This chapter discusses the use of pointers and reference variables, two powerful features of C++ that help to give it the edge over other languages. You will also be introduced to a few lesser-used techniques that build on the basic material you have already covered. Although some of these concepts can be hard to grasp at first, their importance and relevance will become clear as the programs you deal with become more and more complex.

9.1 Memory access through pointers

Like houses on a street, each byte of computer memory is numbered, and has a unique numerical address. When you declare a variable, an address in memory is assigned a name by which the program can refer to it. This system is an improvement over flat numerical addressing because the names can help to describe what the variable is used for, and they are easier to remember. However, referring to areas of memory by name alone is not always ideal – there are certain situations where plain numbering is more useful. To draw an example from the housing analogy, you can guess which house is next door to number 28, but you have no way of knowing who's next door to 'Rose Cottage'.

Fortunately, C++ provides a way of switching between variable names and addresses whenever necessary, and also provides for a new kind of variable, a *pointer*, which is specifically used to hold numerical memory addresses. Pointers are declared like normal variables, except that an asterisk precedes the name.

pointer declaration syntax:

```
type *name;
```

type is any C++ type.

For example:

```
char *pChar;                // a pointer to char
int *pInt1, *pInt2;         // two pointers to integers
float *pfloat, realfloat;   // one pointer, one normal
```

Since pointer variables always store the *address* of some object, they are always the same size, regardless of what they are pointing to. On most machines, a pointer is four bytes long. What, then, does the compiler use the type declaration for? The answer becomes clear as we look further at the capabilities of pointers...

The C++ language handles arithmetic with pointer variables in a very special way. If you add the value '1' to a pointer, the stored address value is not necessarily incremented at the same time. Instead, the pointer address is moved on a sufficient amount to point to the next whole unit in memory. Thus, if the pointer is of type **char** (one byte) the pointer is moved to the next byte in memory. On the other hand, adding one to a pointer-to-float moves the pointer *four* bytes along to the start of the next float. Of course, unless you have specifically declared it to be so, the next group of four bytes does not necessarily correspond to a **float** variable in your code. The listing below demonstrates this mechanism:

```
/* pointer1.cpp (30/9/1999)
declaring and using pointers */

#include <stdio.h>

int integer1 = 1, integer2 = 2;

int main()
{
    // declare a pointer-to-an-integer
    int* pInt;

    // store the address of integer1 in pInt, then print results
    pInt = &integer1;
    printf("Addr: %u, Value: %i\n", pInt, *pInt);

    // move pInt along by one integer space, then reprint results
    pInt++;
    printf("Addr: %u, Value: %i\n", pInt, *pInt);

    return 0;
}
```

Compile and run this program now! On my machine, the output looks like this:

```
Addr: 170, Value: 1
Addr: 172, Value: 2
```

You will probably find that the address numbers are different for you, as you have a different computer set-up. Memory-resident programs, hardware details, and compiler choice will all affect the outcome, but the raw values don't matter. Let's break down the program to see what's going on:

```
int integer1 = 1, integer2 = 2;
```

We declare two integers, and make them global because this guarantees that they will be contiguous – **integer2** comes straight after **integer1** in memory. Local variables are allocated in a different order because the compiler must be able to create and delete them every time the function is called, although we could use the **static** type modifier to force the variables to behave as if they were declared globally. Anyway, what we now have is a four-byte block of memory, where the first pair is named **integer1** and the second pair is named **integer2**.

```
int *pInt;
pInt = &integer1;
```

The first line of the **main** function declares a local pointer-to-integer called **pInt**. Although it is not essential, pointer names are usually given a 'p' prefix to help anyone reading the code to differentiate them from normal variables. Next we copy the *address* of **integer1** to **pInt** using the referencing operator, the ampersand, **&**. This operator simply returns the address of its single operand, so we are using it here to get the address of **integer1** before assigning it to **pInt** in the normal way.

```
printf("Addr: %u, Value: %i\n", pInt, *pInt);
```

The call to **printf** displays first the contents of **pInt** itself, and then the value of the integer (in this case **integer1**) that it points to. To get this second number, we use the dereferencing operator, an asterisk,*. As the name suggests, this operator does the exact opposite of the referencing operator; it converts from an address to a real value. Since **pInt** points to **integer1**, and **integer1** holds the value 1, ***pInt** also evaluates to 1. In general, **A** is equal to *(&A)*, and modifying **A** modifies *(&A)* and vice versa.

This means that having a pointer to a variable is as good as having the name itself for reading and writing to it.

```
pInt++;
printf("Addr: %u, Value: %i\n", pInt, *pInt);
```

We increment **pInt** and print the result. When you run the program, you see that incrementing the pointer actually changed its value by 2, because integers are two bytes long. Now, **pInt** points to the byte directly after those occupied by **integer1**, which we know belongs to **integer2**. This fact is confirmed because *pInt now has the value 2, which is exactly what we initialized **integer2** with in the beginning. In other words, if *pInt returns the value of **integer1**, *(pInt+1) returns the value of **integer2**. The system works because of the special interpretation of pointer arithmetic; the instruction **pInt++;** actually changed **pInt** from 170 to 172.

Note that although we have displayed the addresses as unsigned decimal numbers using the **%u** flag, memory addresses are conventionally counted in hexadecimal. Try changing the **%u** to a **%x** (hex) or **%p** (pointer).

9.2 Pointers in use

Read over that last section another time. Let it sink in a little. Pointer notation is notoriously confusing to beginners, but it will soon come naturally to you. When you're ready to move on, consider this – the name of an array, without any square brackets following, is actually a pointer to the first element. You picked that up in Chapter 4, but if you think about it in the context of what you have just learnt, an interesting relationship appears. The very fact that an array is a contiguous collection of variables makes it ideal for use with pointers.

Consider:

```
char message[] = "Hello";
```

message	is the same as	**&message[0]**
		i.e. **&(message[0])**
(message+1)	is the same as	**&message[1]**
*(message+2)	is the same as	**message[2]**

or even more confusingly…

(message+1)[0]	is the same as	**message[1]**
(message+2)[2]	is the same as	**message[4]**

in general:

(pointer)[number]	is the same as	***(pointer+number)**

The bottom line is that array notation and pointer notation are just two ways of achieving the same thing; the only real difference is that the array system returns values (unless you reference them) and the pointer system returns addresses (unless you dereference them). This association is most apparent with functions that work with arrays – you will notice that their arguments declare *pointers* to type. The **strrev** function in the Standard Library looks something like this:

```
char* strrev(char* str);
```

The function takes an array of characters as its argument, reverses them, and returns the result. What you are actually passing to the function is not the entire string, but the address of the first letter. This is obviously far more efficient, especially with strings that are several hundred characters long. However, it does mean that in general, passing any pointer to a function effectively gives that portion of code full read-write access to your own local or global data. Used carefully this can be a powerful tool, but it does mean you have to be even more careful in designing the program.

Pass-by-pointer, as it is called, is not restricted only to arrays; it can be used whenever a function must be able to modify data that belongs to the calling scope. For instance, the **scanf** function writes user input directly into the program's local variables – it can do this because the address of a suitable variable is passed to it:

```
float fraction;
printf("\nPlease enter a fraction: ");
scanf("%f", &fraction);
...
```

This snippet from Chapter 7 was originally used to show how **scanf** worked, but is a good example of a situation where pass-by-pointer is ideal. Writing your own functions that accept pointers is as simple as listing the arguments appropriately:

```
// function takes a char pointer, an int pointer and
// returns a float pointer
float* myfunc(char* string, int* pInt);
```

Of course, you can use any combination of pointers and plain variables in the argument list of a function. It is normal for the small primitive types (even long doubles) to be passed by value except in cases where the function needs to modify them directly. Arrays, on the other hand, must always be passed by pointer because this is the only way to achieve the desired result; you cannot pass an entire array as a normal function argument. Structures and unions can be passed either by value or by pointer, but since they are usually fairly large, it is more efficient to use a pointer. Many of the more complex functions that make up the Windows API need so many parameters that the only efficient way to call them is to fill out all the members of a giant dedicated structure and then pass a pointer to it. For instance, the Win32 *GetTextMetrics* function takes a pointer to a TEXTMETRIC structure which has no less than 20 different members! Fortunately, in this case it is the function itself that fills out all the information, not the poor programmer...

Functions that return pointers present the interesting possibility of *this* kind of code:

```
int* getpointer(char* name);
...
*(getpointer("James")) = 24;
```

Although the static values returned by normal functions are strictly read-only, it is perfectly legal to write to an *address* that is returned as a pointer. In the code above, the imaginary function **getpointer** takes the name of, say, a data record, and returns a pointer to an integer. Then, via the dereferencing operator, we use that pointer in an assignment expression – it looks strange, but it's legal. In fact, this is the only situation where a function return becomes an assignable *l-value*.

Since all pointer variables are the same size, it is usually fairly safe to cast between, say, pointer-to-double and pointer-to-int; you will only start to encounter problems if you try pointer arithmetic, forgetting that the byte increment will have changed. In fact, just as you can declare a function that returns nothing, you can declare a pointer that points to nothing using the keyword **void**:

```
void *pBuffer = NULL; // NULL is just zero but is used to
mean "empty pointer"
```

This *void pointer* is particularly useful as a function argument because the compiler will happily cast any other pointer to **void** without warning. However, since the variable **pBuffer** has no type, any attempt to add or subtract from it will give a compiler error something like '*void* : unknown or zero size*'. The functions in **memory.h** use void pointers precisely because they are designed to deal with raw memory; the calling program can pass pointers to arrays, structures or void objects and the compiler will not complain.

9.3 Reference variables

The pointer model has been around since the introduction of C, but C++ added a third way to refer to objects in memory. A reference variable is a hybrid between a pointer and a normal object, as you will see:

```
/* refs.cpp (30/9/1999)
reference variables */

#include <iostream.h>

int main()
{
    // declare an integer and a reference-to-an-integer
    int real = 0;
    int& fake = real;

    // print the values of both variables

    cout << "Real: " << real << ", Fake: " << fake << "\n";

    // modify the integer variable and print values again
    real = 1;
    cout << "Real: " << real << ", Fake: " << fake << "\n";

    // modify the reference variable and print values again
    fake = 2;
    cout << "Real: " << real << ", Fake: " << fake << "\n";

    return 0;

}
```

Here's the output:

```
Real: 0, Fake: 0
Real: 1, Fake: 1
Real: 2, Fake: 2
```

At first glance, the only odd thing about this program is the ampersand in the second line of the **main** function – if you didn't know better, you'd say it was a misprint, but in fact, it's of crucial importance. The & symbol makes the variable **fake** a reference variable, just as an asterisk in that position would make it a pointer. The general syntax is:

reference declaration syntax:

```
type& name = variable;
```

type   is any C++ type

variable   is the name of another normal variable of that type

So what then does a reference variable actually do? The object **fake** that we created in the example above is effectively an *alias* for the variable **real**. You already know that a variable declaration gives a name to a certain area of memory; what is now happening is that a *new* name is being given to the *same* block of memory. This partnership is demonstrated by the program – changing the value of **real** simultaneously changes the value of **fake**, and vice-versa. Why? Because both names represent the same two bytes of memory. If you want to convince yourself of this, modify the program so that it prints both **&real** and **&fake**. You will see that the two addresses are identical.

The reference variable has interesting properties because it combines elements of both traditional and pointer-based memory handling. Reference variables are used just like the normal variables that you met way back in Chapter 2, but the way that one object can be an alias for another is more pointer-like – you saw earlier that (*pointer) is effectively an alias for the variable that is pointed to. However, you are probably still unconvinced that reference variables have any practical use – why have fake when you can have real? The answer is that references come into their own when used as function arguments, a system called pass-by-reference:

```
/* passrefs.cpp (30/9/1999)
using pass-by-reference */
```

```
#include <iostream.h>
int reciprocal(double& x);
int main()
{
    double number = 0.50;

    // prompt the user for a number to use
    cout << "Enter a double: "; cin >> number;
    cout << "The number is: " << number << "\n";

    // call the reciprocal function to modify number directly
    if (!reciprocal(number))
        cout << "Error! reciprocal function failed."; // 0 returned
    else
        cout << "Reciprocal is: " << number << "\n";  // 1 returned

    return 0;
}
// calculate reciprocal of a number with error-checking,
// returning 'true' or 'false' to indicate success of failure
int reciprocal(double& x)
{
    if (x)
    {
        // if 'x' is non-zero, modify it and return 'true'
        x = 1 / x;
        return 1;
    }
    // 'x' is zero, so return 'false'
    return 0;
}
```

Output:

```
Enter a double: 6.98412345
The number is: 6.984123
Reciprocal is: 0.143182
```

Here's an example of a function that uses a reference argument. As you can see, it finds the reciprocal of a number by performing the calculation 1/x. However, since we have to divide by x the value cannot be zero, so we check that it isn't using an **if** statement. If x is non-zero and the function succeeds, it returns 1 (true). If x is zero the function fails, returning 0 (false). Notice that we don't need an **else** clause here because under normal operation the **return 1;** statement ends the function within the **if** block, so **return 0;** is only reached if **x** is zero.

Now, here's the clever part: the argument **x** is a reference, which means that when the variable **number** is passed to **reciprocal** by **main**, **x** becomes an *alias* for **number**. Thus, every modification of **x** within the **reciprocal** function affects the variable that was passed to it by the caller. You can see that this is the case because when the value of **number** is printed later on, it has changed. What's significant here is that **number** is local to the **main** function and yet can still be modified by **reciprocal**. This is a far neater solution than, for example, declaring a variable globally, and it avoids the hassle of referencing and dereferencing that is incurred by the pass-by-pointer method. Pass-by-reference is also more efficient: If one of the arguments to a function was a large structure, passing it by reference would save the overhead of making a new copy, but the function is still called in exactly the same way. There is an added danger, though, because inadvertent modification within the function will affect the object in the calling function that was passed as an argument.

9.4 Miscellaneous features

This section details a collection of minor language elements that I have not had the opportunity to introduce until now. You may not use these techniques all the time, but you are likely to encounter them in somebody else's code if not your own.

Default arguments to functions

If you are writing a function that is likely to be called with the same arguments over and over again, it is worth specifying a set of defaults. To do so, the function definition is changed so that the default values appear after the arguments like this:

```
void function(int one = 1, float two = 0.98, double three = 3.456)
{
    ...
}
```

A function with defaults can be called in a number of different ways:

```
function();              // use all three defaults
function(10);            // use 0.98 and 3.456 as defaults
function(10, 1.23f);        // use just 3.456 by default
function(10, 1.23f, 0.9412);  // no defaults used
```

In order for the compiler to know what argument goes where, there must be a clear division between required and optional arguments. If you specify a single argument, it is automatically assumed to be intended for the first in the list, which is **int one** in this case; if you specify two arguments, they map to **int one** and **float two**. Because each argument relies on having the previous ones filled in too, you should declare the less-important arguments towards the end of the list. The same principle extends to functions with a combination of required and optional arguments – all the arguments without defaults must appear first to avoid ambiguity when calling the function:

```
void function2(int one, int two, int three = 1, int four = 0)
{
    ...
}
```

This function can be called with two, three or four arguments.

The difference between i++ and ++i

The increment and decrement operators ++ and -- take effect at different times depending on whether they appear before or after their operand. If you put the operator in front, the increment/decrement occurs *before* the rest of the expression is evaluated; if you put it behind, the increment/decrement occurs *after* the expression is evaluated. In other words, you either get the new value or the old value of a variable depending on the position of the operator:

```
/* incdec.cpp (30/9/1999)
difference between i++ and ++i */

#include <stdio.h>

int main()
{
    int A = 5, B = 10;
    printf("Startup A,B - %i, %i\n", A, B);
```

```
A = B++; // same as A = B; B++;
printf("After A=B++ - %i, %i\n", A, B);

A = ++B; // same as B++; A = B;
printf("After A=++B - %i, %i\n", A, B);

return 0;
}
```

Here's the output – study it carefully.

```
Startup A,B - 5, 10
After A=B++ - 10, 11
After A=++B - 12, 12
```

After the first operation, **A** is 10 and **B** is 11. The increment on **B** occurred after that part of the expression was evaluated, so **A** gets the previous value. After the second operation, **A** and **B** are both 12. The increment on **B** occurred before that part of the expression was evaluated, so **A** got the new value of **B**. The effect on **B** was the same both times, but the result of the expression was different.

The asm keyword

You can use the **asm** keyword to embed assembler code directly into your source code, which is useful when the C++ alternative is either inefficient or non-existent. Of course, you need to have a good understanding of assembly language and the x86 instruction set before you even attempt this, so from here on in I will assume that you do.

Assembler statements can use any C++ variable and function names that are in scope, in addition to the usual register symbols and instruction mnemonics. Don't forget that in C++ hex constants are marked by a preceding '0x' rather than the usual 'h' suffix. Statements are terminated by the end of the line or a semicolon, and must either be prefixed with the **asm** keyword or be surrounded by an **asm** block:

```
// single line statement
asm int 0x19

// block asm statement
asm
{
```

```
        mox ax, 0x2b16
        mov cx, 0x0643
        int 0x21

}
```

You need not preserve EAX, EBX, ECX or EDX across an inline **asm** block, so the example above will not create any problems. It is usually safe to change ESI and EDI too, unless the compiler is running an incompatible optimization routine – check the documentation.

At the end of a function the compiler automatically generates *epilogue code* to clean up the stack and return, so you should not include a **ret** instruction in your own assembler code. To return an integer value, set AX in the assembler block and omit the C++ **return** statement; this will generate a harmless compiler warning but will allow the value in AX to be returned to the caller. Alternatively, you can define the function with the **naked** attribute, which disables prologue and epilogue generation. You must pop the function arguments off the stack yourself and adjust for local variable space if you do this.

Here's a quick demo – the program calls int 33h to get basic information on the mouse driver. Some implementations have a function called **int86** which you could use to call the interrupt instead; but it's almost quicker with **asm** anyway:

```
/* asm.cpp (30/9/1999)
using asm keyword */
#include <stdio.h>
#include <string.h>
int main()
{
    char major, minor, type, intrpt;
    char typename[15], portname[15];
    asm
    {
        mov ax, 0x0024
        int 0x33
        mov major, bh
        mov minor, bl
        mov type, ch
        mov intrpt, cl
    }
```

```
switch(type)
{
case 1:
   strcpy(typename, "Bus");
   break;
case 2:
   strcpy(typename, "Serial");
   break;
case 3:
   strcpy(typename, "InPort");
   break;
case 4:
   strcpy(typename, "PS/2");
   break;
default:
   strcpy(typename, "Non-Standard");
}
if (intrpt == 0)
   strcpy(portname, "AUX");
else
   sprintf(portname, "IRQ%u", intrpt);

printf("\nMouse Driver Version %x.%x", major, minor);
printf("\nType: %s Mouse on %s.\n", typename, portname);

return 0;
}
```

On my machine, the integral pointer driver reports this:

```
Mouse Driver Version 8.30
Type: PS/2 Mouse on AUX.
```

The extern keyword

If you have several source files in your project, each one will need to access variables and functions declared and defined in the others. To allow this, you must re-declare functions and variables at the beginning of each file using the **extern** keyword:

```
// re-declare external objects for use in this file...
extern int getnumber();
extern char forename[], surname[];
extern int x, y, z;
```

You cannot initialize variables declared with **extern** because no memory is allocated for them here; it is the source file in which they are declared that handles allocation and initialization. Since the compiler has no knowledge of external source, object and library files, it is the linker that will actually try to find these variables. You can test this behaviour with the following two source files:

```
/* extmain.cpp (30/9/1999)
testing external linkage
main program file */

#include <iostream.h>

// this integer is declared somewhere else
extern int externalnumber;
int main()
{
    // print the value as normal
    cout << externalnumber;
    return 0;
}
```

End of **extmain.cpp** – start of **extdecl.cpp**

```
/* extdecl.cpp (30/9/1999)
testing external linkage
secondary source file */

// declare and initialize a global integer
int externalnumber = 3;
```

To get these two files to link together as a single program, you will probably need to create a new project in your IDE. Save both source files, then add to them to the project using the appropriate menu option. Command-line users will need to compile both sources and then link them with **link extmain.obj extdecl.obj**, or something similar.

When the program runs, the external integer **externalnumber** is printed to the screen. If you open up **extdecl.cpp**, add a typo to the name of the variable and rebuild, the linker should give an error of the form

Linker Error: undefined symbol _externalnumber in module EXTMAIN.CPP

This occurs because the symbol **externalnumber** that you have declared in **extmain.cpp** is now nowhere to be found in any of the specified object code.

Summary

We have seen that pointers and reference variables can provide powerful solutions to many memory accessing problems. The referencing and dereferencing operators convert between names and addresses, and the increment and decrement operators take on special meanings when used with pointers. You have seen that pointer notation and array notation are actually two ways of handling the same basic situation; when you have a pointer to a list of values, you can use pointer arithmetic and any combination of **&**, * and [ ] to get the result you need.

Pointers and references can be used as function arguments, to allow modification of the variable that was passed, or to avoid the inefficiency of creating extra copies. Although large structures can be passed by value, they are usually passed by pointer for this reason. You can also use a generic void pointer as a function argument, to allow implicit casting of function arguments.

You saw how to create functions with one or more optional arguments, which are subject to certain ordering rules which are necessary to avoid ambiguities. You know how to use the extern keyword to access variables and functions declared in external source files, and if you're an assembly nut, you'll be relieved to have learnt how to embed assembly language into your C++ source code using **asm** blocks.

Exercises

1   Find any program from an earlier exercise that uses arrays, and modify it so that only pointer notation is used – in other words, square brackets are banned.

2   Take the code from Chapter 6, Exercise 3 and convert it to a stand-alone module that can be linked in with another program and called as necessary. Test it.

10 object-oriented programming

In this chapter you will learn

- how to construct your first OOP program
- the difference between public and private variables
- how to re-define the C++ operators for your own use

Aims of this chapter

Object-oriented programming, or OOP, is an approach to software design that emphasizes the structure of a problem rather than the logic required to solve it. This chapter introduces the philosophy and jargon behind OOP and goes on to describe its implementation in C++.

10.1 The aims of OOP

OOP was created in an effort to deal with the ever-growing complexity of software, and the difficulty in expanding and customizing existing systems. Put simply, OOP does not give an end result that appears, to the user at least, any different from what could be achieved using 'ordinary' code – what it does do is revolutionize the way the source code is written and the program is structured internally. How? With OOP, the traditional view of variables, functions and conditional structures is moved aside in favour of an entirely object-oriented approach. By doing it this way, real-life entities are easier to simulate, the code is inherently more modular, and bugs are reduced because access is restricted to the allowable channels.

10.2 OOP jargon

OOP defines an *object* in a very accurate way:

- Objects can contain variables, known as *data members*, and functions, known as *member functions*. Other languages refer to the data members as *fields* and the member functions as *methods*.

- The members of an object (its data and functions) can be declared *private*, *protected*, or *public*. These *access specifiers* are used to regulate access to the object's members from outside.

- Objects can be derived from other objects. When this is done, the new object can *inherit* the base class members, as well as defining its own new ones. An object can have any number of 'parents' – this is known as multiple inheritance.

The keywords **class**, **struct** and **union** are all described as object types, but there is some confusion about what is and is not an object. In plain C, **struct** and **union** existed solely to group data – they could not have member functions or access specifiers, and they could not be derived from others. In C++, unions are still the same, but structures can now have all the important features of a true object. On top of that, the **class** keyword was introduced. It is the same as **struct**, except that the members of a structure are public by default, while the members of a class are private by default. For this reason, programmers tend to use **struct** in its old C role for grouping variables, and **class** for creating fully-fledged objects complete with member functions. I will tend to discuss classes rather than structures because there is no ambiguity with the old C definition, but they are, however, almost interchangeable.

10.3 Defining an object

The definition syntax for objects has several component parts:

```
classkey name : baselist
{
access specifiers:
    memberlist;
} instancelist;
```

classkey	either 'class' or 'struct'
name	the name of this new object
baselist	optional list of parent objects
access specifiers	optional labels 'private', 'protected' or 'public'
memberlist	declarations of member functions and data
instancelist	optional list of instances to create

You will also need to write the body code for each of the member functions that you specified in the definition. The functions definitions can appear anywhere in the source code, so long as the class itself has been defined first, and the only difference from a normal function definition is the first line, which must now include the name of the class for which the function is a member. If, for example, you have defined a class **MyClass** and declared member function **int MemberFunc()**, you would define **MemberFunc** like this:

```
int MyClass::MemberFunc()
{
    ...
}
```

Because it is a member, the function can access all other members of **MyClass**, including those declared private, as well as the 'normal' functions available from any part of the source code. If you accidentally omit the **MyClass::** part of the function definition, the file will still compile without errors, but not the way you wanted it to. It is legal to have a member function of a class with the same name as one that is declared globally. The compiler will create a normal **MemberFunc** that is not a member of any class, and since the version of **MemberFunc** that is a member of **MyClass** has already been declared in the class definition, the compiler will assume that the function code is another file. Only when you try to link the code will an error occur, because no code for **MyClass::MemberFunc** will be found in any of the object or library files.

10.4   Using the new class

Now that you have a complete class definition, you can create and use instances of that class in your source code. The class must be defined in every source file that you use it in, so the definition is often put in a separate header file that can be included wherever necessary. The definitions of the member functions, however, need only be compiled once. A small object-oriented program might have the following structure:

classdef.h	Definition of all the classes
clsfunc.cpp	Definition, or implementation, of class member functions
appmain.cpp	Main program; creates and uses instances of the classes

Classdef.h would be included in both of the .cpp files, which is efficient as the definition of an object takes little or no code. The implementation – the member function code – is what uses space in the .exe file, and the instances of the class are what use memory at run time.

If **classdef.h** contained the single class **CVehicle** it might look like this:

```
/* classdef.h (30/9/1999)
definition of CVehicle */

#ifndef CLASS_VEHICLE
#define CLASS_VEHICLE

class CVehicle   // no base classes
{
// these members are accessible only from within the class
private:
    unsigned int weight, capacity;
    float topspeed;

// these members are accessible from anywhere in the program
public:
    void printdata();
}; // no instances created here
#endif
```

Clsfunc.cpp contains the function definitions:

```
/* clsfunc.cpp (30/9/1999)
implementation of CVehicle */

#include "classdef.h"
#include <stdio.h>

void CVehicle::printdata()
{
    printf("Weight: %u, Capacity: %u, Top Speed: %f\n",
        weight, capacity, topspeed);
}
```

What we have here is the skeleton for a class called **CVehicle** that models some basic properties of a real vehicle. The private data members represent three real-life properties (weight, passenger capacity and top speed) and the **printdata** function lets us dump the values to the screen. Since the design of the class prevents direct access to the data members, we have already started to impose strict control over the use of the class. It is this discipline that makes the OOP model so useful for large, unwieldy projects – information is accessible on an exacting 'need-to-know' basis.

Meanwhile, **appmain.cpp** contains the **main** function which creates an instance of **CVehicle** and calls the member function **printdata**.

```
/* appmain.cpp (30/9/1999)
test program for CVehicle */

#include "classdef.h"

int main()
{
    // create an instance of CVehicle called mycar
    CVehicle mycar;

    // call CVehicle::printdata in mycar
    mycar.printdata();

    return 0;
}
```

The output of **appmain.exe** looks like this:

```
Weight: 0, Capacity: 0, Top Speed: 0.000000
```

Since the data members of **mycar** have not yet been initialized, the **printdata** function outputs all zeroes. In the next section, we will discuss the different ways of allowing for initialization of class data without compromising the security structure already in place.

Notice the use of the direct member selection operator, a stop mark, in the second statement of **main**. Its purpose is simply to specify which member of the given object instance you are trying to access, just as you used it for structures and unions in Chapter 5. The difference is that now you can use it to call member functions as well, although the **printdata** function must be declared **public** to be accessed in this way. If, instead, you have a pointer to an object instance, you could use the dereferencing operator to achieve the same result as before, like this:

```
// pcar points to object mycar
(*pcar).printdata();
```

However, C++ provides a neater way of doing this, with the indirect member selection operator, which looks like an arrow. So, the line above is usually written like this:

```
car->printdata();
```

These operators are also used to access the data members of classes, structs and unions, but again, only if they have been declared public (explicitly or by default). In addition, the .* operator is available for dereferencing pointers to class members, and the ->* operator for dereferencing pointers to pointers to class members.

10.5 get* and set* functions

Private data members are useful not because they disallow external access entirely, but because they can be used to control the kind of access that a program has to the members of a class. To achieve this, each important private data member is often accompanied by a pair of simple public functions that provide facilities to get and to set the data as required. Rather than allowing indiscriminate access to a variable (by declaring it public) a class that combines private members with public **get/set** functions effectively creates a single, controlled channel through which an application can safely access its information.

We'll expand the **CVehicle** class to include some get/set functions for the three private members. The **get*** functions could be declared like this in the **public** section of **CVehicle**:

```
// get a copy of the private data member 'weight'
unsigned int getWeight();
// get a copy of the private data member 'capacity'
unsigned int getCapacity();
// get a copy of the private data member 'topspeed'
float getTopspeed();
```

For each of these functions, the definition in **clsfunc.cpp** would simply follow this form:

```
unsigned int CVehicle::getWeight()
{
    return weight;
}
```

Since **get*** functions are very often just one-liners, programmers often make use of a special kind of function called an *inline function*. The body code of these functions is substituted directly into the program code each time they are called – a system that may slightly improve the speed of your program at the expense of the executable file size. Most **get*** functions typically contain only a single statement, so they are ideal candidates for this kind of optimization, because it is likely that the invisible overhead of entering and exiting the function actually takes more processor time than the function code itself.

Although you can use the **inline** keyword to explicitly declare an inline function, class member functions can be made inline automatically if you place the function body directly after the declaration within the class:

```
// these get* functions are implicitly inline
unsigned int getWeight() { return weight; }
unsigned int getCapacity() { return capacity; }
float getTopspeed() { return topspeed; }
```

If your **get*** functions are declared this way, there's no need to define a function body separately in **clsfunc.cpp**, because all the code has already been written straight into the class declaration.

The accompanying **set*** functions are usually a little more complex because if they are to be of any use, they must include code to check that the input is valid before assigning it to the private data member in question. This declaration of the weight-setting function demonstrates the form for the others:

```
unsigned int setWeight(unsigned int new_wt);
```

You can build as much input-checking as you need into your **set*** functions, but a simple range check is usually sufficient for most situations. Here's a prototype definition that you could add to **clsfunc.cpp**:

```
unsigned int CVehicle::setWeight(unsigned int new_wt)
{
    unsigned int temp = weight;

    // check the input value and quit if it's unsuitable
    if ((new_wt <= 0) || (new_wt > 1000)) return 0;
```

```
// assign the new value and return the previous one
    weight = new_wt;
    return temp;
}
```

It's my gut feeling that a **set*** function such as this is probably not worth inlining, but you could consult your compiler documentation for notes about when and when not to use the inline specifier. The important thing is that we have now created a safe mode of access to the private members of the **CVehicle** class.

10.6 Friends

In more complicated OOP structures, it is often convenient to create specific access channels between two inherently unrelated objects. To do this, a class must invite additional objects or functions to take access to its private members by declaring *friends*.

If we had a **CWeatherSystem** class, we could modify the **CVehicle** class to allow the weather object to modify the vehicle's private characteristics, just as real rain and wind might affect a car's top speed:

```
class CVehicle
{
    friend class CWeatherSystem;
private:
    unsigned int weight, capacity;
    float topspeed;
public:
    void printdata();
};
```

Although **CVehicle.topspeed** is still inaccessible to conventional functions, those that are members of **CWeatherSystem** can now read and write to it as normal. Friendship is not mutual in the C++ model, so for **CVehicle** members to access private **CWeatherSystem** members would mean **CWeatherSystem** returning the favour by declaring **CVehicle** a friend. In the further interests of security, friendship exists only where it is explicitly declared; that is, inherited classes lose any of the links their parents had, and friendship can not be conveyed across successive relationships. This means that neither children, nor friends, of **CWeatherSystem** have access to **CVehicle**'s members even though **CWeatherSystem** is itself a friend of **CVehicle**.

As a starting point for the **CWeatherSystem** class we might create some private members to hold various environmental factors, and a public member function to exert some influence on a **CVehicle** object:

```
// in classdef.h
class CWeatherSystem
{
private:
    float windspeed, rainrate, sunlight;
public:
    int apply(CVehicle* pTarget);
} local_weather;
```

The three floating-point variables will contain notional quantities of their respective weather elements, and the **apply** function will modify the CVehicle object passed to it by a pointer. Since the program is likely to use one and only one instance of the class, the declaration automatically creates an instance called **local_weather**.

```
// in clsfunc.cpp
CWeatherSystem::apply(CVehicle* pTarget)
{
    // check the pointer and quit if necessary
    if (!pTarget) return 0;

    // modify some of the CVehicle's private data,
    // based on a calculation from our own data.
    pTarget->topspeed /= ((1 – rainrate) * (20 - windspeed));

    // return 'true'
    return 1;
}
```

The skeletal **CWeatherSystem::apply** function shown above returns a true-or-false value depending on the success of the operation. The first line makes sure that **pTarget** is not a null pointer; the second line makes an arbitrary modification of the target CVehicle instance's private **topspeed** variable. This mechanism is only possible because CWeatherSystem is a friend of CVehicle, which allows it access to the private data. The appmain.cpp file shown previously could call the **apply** function with a line of the form "local_weather.apply(&mycar);".

10.7 Construction and destruction

The C++ object model is made more flexible by its provision for customized initialization and exit functions. Data members cannot be initialized when they are declared because the class definition itself does not occupy memory – it is the instances that are actually created and stored in memory. To perform initialization then, you must declare a special function called a *constructor*. If you do not specify your own, the compiler creates a 'blank' one automatically.

Constructors are member functions that are distinguished from the rest by the fact that they have the same name as the class, and they have no return type – not even void. The compiler calls the constructor automatically whenever a new instance of the object is created. You can also declare *destructors*, which are called when an instance is destroyed. Destructors are identified by a tilde (~) followed by the class name, and they too have no return type. As long as they all take different argument types, any number of constructors can be declared, but you can only declare one destructor.

The class **CVehicle** could be expanded to include custom initialization and termination by adding a few lines in the class definition. Constructors and destructors must be declared **public** or they won't be accessible to whoever is trying to create a new instance of the class. Add these lines to **classdef.h** directly below the declaration of **void printdata()**:

```
// declare two constructors and a destructor
CVehicle();
CVehicle(int new_wt, int new_cap, float new_tspd);
~CVehicle();
```

Once declared in the class definition, the contructors and destructors are defined in the same way as normal member functions, except that there is no type keyword in the first line. Add the following definitions to **clsfunc.cpp**:

```
// constructor 1: set data members to zero
CVehicle::CVehicle()
{
    topspeed = weight = capacity = 0;
    printf("Object Created.\n");
}

// constructor 2: initialize data members with supplied arguments
CVehicle::CVehicle(int new_wt, int new_cap, float new_tspd)
{
    weight = new_wt;
    capacity = new_cap;
    topspeed = new_tspd;
    printf("Object Created & Initialized.\n");
}

// destructor: print message and quit
CVehicle::~CVehicle()
{
    printf("Object Destroyed.\n");
}
```

The compiler can tell which constructor to use by the arguments being passed to it. The previous example provides two – one that would use the default values, and one allowing user-specified values. Using a constructor with arguments is like calling a function, except that for constructors with no arguments at all, you do not supply the empty parentheses as you would in a normal function call. For example:

```
/* appmain.cpp [revision 2] (30/9/1999)
test program for CVehicle */

#include "classdef.h"

int main()
{
    // create two instances
    CVehicle mycar1;
    CVehicle mycar2(10000, 4, 124.5f);

    // print the data
    mycar1.printdata();
```

```
    mycar2.printdata();
    return 0;
}
```

The destructor is used to perform any cleanup required before
the instance of the object is closed. This is particularly significant if any other member function allocated memory using
the **new** operator. If the destructor does not delete it, the
memory will not be reclaimed by the system until the program
ends. If objects are created and destroyed frequently, the program will eventually fail due to lack of free memory. If you run
this updated version of the program, you should see this:

```
Object Created.
Object Created & Initialized.
Weight: 0, Capacity: 0, Top Speed: 0.000000
Weight: 10000, Capacity: 4, Top Speed: 124.500000
Object Destroyed.
Object Destroyed.
```

The '*Object Destroyed*' message appears twice because the
destructor is automatically called for both instances of **CVehicle**
when they go out of scope (i.e. when the **main** function ends).

10.8 Overloading operators

Just as the C++ language provides a wealth of operators for
working with the basic types, class definitions can include 'operator overloads' that specify how a given operator behaves in
conjunction with this new object. Any operator can be overloaded, except for ., .*, :: and ?:. Operator overloads are really
a special kind of function, but instead of the function name,
the keyword **operator** is used, followed by the operator that
you wish to overload. The operator that you use effectively
becomes the function's name.

Before you choose just any old symbol, remember that you
must use a combination of characters that is already a C++
operator. Thus, <<< is not acceptable but << is, because it
usually acts as the bitwise left shift operator. You should consider, too, whether the operator you are overloading would
normally have any meaning when used in conjunction with an
instance of your class. For example, most of the arithmetic
operators are safe to overload because they have no meaning

when applied to a user-defined object. You must also decide whether you want an operator that takes two operands (a *binary* operator) or one that takes only one (a *unary* operator).

Whether you choose a binary or a unary operator, there are two ways of declaring the overload – it can be done entirely outside the class definition, or it can be declared as a member of the class, and then defined like a normal member function. In the latter case, the first operand is assumed to be the class instance itself.

As an example, we can add an operator to **CVehicle** – a customized version of the addition operator +. For **CVehicle**, we will define the sum of two **CVehicle** objects as a single **CVehicle** object whose parameters are the sum of the respective parameters of two operands added together. Of course, the symbol + can have whatever meaning you like.

To declare an operator overload takes this code:

operator keyword syntax:

```
type operator symbol (arglist)
{
    statements;
    return type;
}
```

type   the type which the operator expression will return

operator identifies this function as an overload

symbol   the symbol for the operator to be overloaded

arglist   either zero, one or two arguments for the operator.

As it is often necessary to access the protected members of a class within the operator function, overloads are usually declared friends of the relevant classes, or declared within the class itself.

We'll start by declaring the + overload outside the class definition. Since + is a binary operator, it has two operands, so there will be two arguments to the operator function. The first one corresponds to the left-hand argument; the second one to the right-hand argument:

```
CVehicle operator + (CVehicle left, CVehicle right);
```

The line shown above would go into **classdef.h** following the declaration of the **CVehicle** class itself. Somewhere *inside* the **CVehicle** declaration, we must add the line

```
friend operator + (CVehicle left, CVehicle right);
```

...to allow the **operator** function to access the private members of the class. All that remains then is to define the actual body of the operator function, which could be placed in either of the two source files in our demo project. Although it is not strictly a member function, the operator overload is very much a part of the object structure, so I'd place it in **clsfunc.cpp**:

```
CVehicle operator + (CVehicle left, CVehicle right)
{
    return CVehicle(left.weight + right.weight,
        left.capacity + right.capacity,
        left.topspeed + right.topspeed);
}
```

It's a simple piece of code – the function just returns a new **CVehicle** object constructed from the data of the two operands in the operator expression. If the operator function wasn't a friend of **CVehicle**, this procedure would be impossible.

The second way to declare operator overloads is to define them as a member of a class. The left-hand operand is assumed to be the class instance itself – that leaves a single argument in the list to represent the right-hand operand. Here's some alternative sample code for the **CVehicle** addition operator – this time it is declared *inside* the public area of the class like this:

```
CVehicle operator + (CVehicle right);
```

It is defined in **clsfunc.cpp** along with the other member functions, like this:

```
CVehicle CVehicle::operator + (CVehicle right)
{
    return CVehicle(weight + right.weight,
        capacity + right.capacity,
        topspeed + right.topspeed);
}
```

As the operator function is within the class this time, it has direct access to its own private **weight**, **capacity** and **topspeed** variables, and it also has access to the private members of the second instance **right**.

You can test either version of the new operator with this third version of **appmain.cpp**:

```
/* appmain.cpp [revision 3] (30/9/1999)
test program for CVehicle with operator overload */

#include "classdef.h"

int main()
{
    // create two instances
    CVehicle mycar1(5000, 2, 139.7f);
    CVehicle mycar2(10000, 4, 124.5f);

    // print the data
    mycar1.printdata();
    mycar2.printdata();
    (mycar1+mycar2).printdata();
    return 0;
}
```

If we include all the additions to CVehicle so far, the class declaration grows into something like this:

```
class CVehicle
{
    // friend declaration (CWeatherSystem must be declared first)
    friend class CWeatherSystem;

private:
    // private data members
    unsigned int weight, capacity;
    float topspeed;

public:
    // constructors
    CVehicle();
    CVehicle(int new_wt, int new_cap, float new_tspd);
    // destructor
    ~CVehicle();

    // operator overload
    CVehicle operator + (CVehicle right);

    // normal member functions
```

```
void printdata();
unsigned int setWeight(unsigned int new_wt);
unsigned int setWeight(unsigned int new_cap);
float setTopspeed(float new_tspd);

// inline get* functions
unsigned int getWeight() { return weight; }
unsigned int getCapacity() { return capacity; }
float getTopspeed() { return topspeed; }
};
```

10.9 Inheritance

Having covered all the major features of a class, the last topic is inheritance. By building carefully-designed class hierarchies, it is possible to create a coding system that is logical, flexible and powerful.

You can derive a class from any number of previously-defined classes by listing their names on the first line of the class definition. Derived classes inherit all overloaded operators and public members of their base classes, and their base classes, and so on. Private members are not inherited – if you want to declare members that are protected from the 'outside world' but are also accessible to derived classes, use the access specifier **protected:**.

Normally, the members inherited by a derived class keep their access attributes – for example, protected members of the base class remain protected in the derived class. However, if you add an access specifier to the list of base classes, the access attributes can be made stricter. This is useful for preventing further classes from being derived from your new base class. For example, to derive a new class **ClassDeriv** from the two classes **Base1** and **Base2**, you might use the following code:

```
class ClassDeriv : public Base1, private Base2
{
    ...
};
```

The preceding **public** means that the access for members of **Base1** remains the same in the derived version. Since **public** is the default derivation method, it can be omitted. The **private** specifier, on the other hand, means that all the inherited members of **Base2** become private in **ClassDeriv**. That means that any classes derived from **ClassDeriv** would not have access to the data or functions inherited from **Base2**, so that part of the heirarchy is effectively cut off. The general rule is this: public derivations leave the access specifiers alone, protected derivations make everything inherited by the derived class protected, and private derivations make everything inherited by the derived class private.

10.10 Constructors and destructors in derived classes

Regardless of the access attributes within their own class, constructors and destructors are never inherited by derived classes. However, whenever an instance of a derived class is created, the constructors for its base classes are called first, so that the structure of objects is built up correctly. In the same way, objects are 'dismantled' correctly when they are destroyed because the destructors of the classes are called in reverse order – derived first, then bases, then their bases, and so on.

Constructors in a derived class can pass arguments on to the base constructors by adding information to the function definition. This allows constructors for derived classes to correctly initialize the base classes even if all the functions for the base classes are already compiled into object code – in other words, you do not need the source code of the implementation of a class to derive your own from it; you only need the definition. This has very useful commercial implications!

Passing data to a base constructor couldn't be simpler. Imagine two base classes:

- **Base1** has a constructor **Base1::Base1(float j_new)**, which initializes the protected member **j** – using a top secret technique – with the new value.

- **Base2** has a constructor **Base2::Base2(char k_new)**, which initializes the protected member **k** in a similar way. We could then derive a new class like this:

```
class Deriv1 : Base1, Base2   // public derivation
{
```

```
    int i;
    Deriv1(int new_i, float new_j, char new_k);
};
```

The constructor definition passes two of its arguments on to the base constructors, thus ensuring that any inherited members are initialized correctly. In the implementation code for **Deriv1**, the constructor could be defined like this:

```
Deriv1::Deriv1(int new_i, float new_j, char new_k) :
    Base1(new_j), Base2(new_k)
{
    i = new_i;
}
```

Notice how the normal argument list is followed by a colon and a list of the base constructors to which you want to pass arguments. You do not have to list all the parent constructors here; only the ones to which you want to push data. In more advanced class heirarchies, this feature can be used to prevent the user from creating instances of classes that are intended solely as bases for others (such a class is known as an abstract class). If the constructors of the base classes are declared protected, the 'outside world' does not have access to the constructors, so no instances of that base class can be created. However, the constructors for the derived classes can still call the base constructors, using the syntax outlined above. Because they are member functions, they have access to the protected constructors of the base classes.

10.11 Virtual functions

You can make a function *virtual* in a base class when you expect derived classes to redefine it. This allows several versions of the same function to coexist; by using the 'virtual' keyword you can ensure that the compiler will use the correct version for the type of instance you're calling it for. The code below defines a class called **CVehicle** and another called **CAirVehicle** that is derived from it:

```
/* virtual.cpp (30/9/1999)
using virtual functions */
#include <iostream.h>
```

```
class CVehicle
{
public:
    virtual void virtfunction() { cout << "CVehicle::Virtual\n"; }
    void nonvirtfunc() { cout << "CVehicle::NonVirtual\n"; }
};

class CAirVehicle : public CVehicle
{
public:
    void virtfunction() { cout << "CAirVehicle::Virtual\n"; }
    void nonvirtfunc() { cout << "CAirVehicle::NonVirtual\n"; }
};

int main()
{
    CAirVehicle airvehicle;

    CVehicle *p_vehicle = &airvehicle;
    CAirVehicle *p_airvehicle = &airvehicle;

    cout << "Calling functions using CAirVehicle pointer...\n";
    p_airvehicle->virtfunction();
    p_airvehicle->nonvirtfunc();

    cout << "Calling functions using CVehicle pointer...\n";
    p_vehicle->virtfunction();
    p_vehicle->nonvirtfunc();

    return 0;
}
```

The first thing you notice is that **CVehicle** defines two functions **virtfunction** and **nonvirtfunc** only to have them *redefined* by **CAirVehicle**. This is all fine so far; instances of CVehicle will call the functions in **CVehicle**, and instances of CAirVehicle will call the functions in **CAirVehicle**. However, the code in **main** puts this system under a bit of stress by using a CVehicle pointer and a CAirVehicle pointer, and referring *both* of them to a CAirVehicle object. This creates an ambiguity; should the line "**p_vehicle->nonvirtfunc**();" call the function in **CVehicle** on the basis that **p_vehicle** is itself a CVehicle pointer, or should it call the function in **CAirVehicle** because **p_vehicle** is pointing to an instance of CAirVehicle? Look at the program's output for the answer:

Calling functions using CAirVehicle pointer...
CAirVehicle::Virtual
CAirVehicle::NonVirtual
Calling functions using CVehicle pointer...
CAirVehicle::Virtual
CVehicle::NonVirtual

The **virtual** keyword used in the declaration of **CVehicle::virtfunction** makes all the difference. When we call the CAirVehicle object's functions through the CAirVehicle pointer, the compiler correctly calls the functions belonging to **CAirVehicle**. However, when calling the CAirVehicle object's functions through the CVehicle pointer, the difference between the virtual and the non-virtual functions becomes apparent. Since we declared **virtfunction** as virtual, the compiler calls the CAirVehicle version even though we are accessing an instance of CAirVehicle *via* CVehicle pointer. Meanwhile, the call to the non-virtual function **nonvirtfunc** gets incorrectly referred back to the CVehicle version, even though the object in question is actually an instance of CAirVehicle. The bottom line is this: if you think a function in a base class may be re-declared in a derived class, you should declare it **virtual** to ensure that the correct version is called, whatever the circumstances.

Summary

This has been a lightning tour of OOP. You saw how to create a basic class with public, protected and private members, and how to create additional links with friend declarations. We looked at the implementation of member functions, including custom constructors and destructors, which have the same name as the class and no return type. You can declare operator overloads to make the new class behave like a normal numerical variable. The syntax is similar to that for a normal member function, except that 'operator [symbol]' replaces the normal name tag. Finally, you were introduced to the concept of inheritance. Class constructors can pass arguments on to their base constructors by calling them at the beginning of the function definition. You can allow multiple redefinitions of a function across the hierarchy by declaring it virtual.

Exercises

1 Implement a subtraction operator overload for CVehicle.

2 Create a new CWarVehicle class that is derived from **CVehicle**. Give it a new protected data member to store, say, armour thickness or weapon stocks. Include constructors and destructors that print status messages (like those for CVehicle) and add **get*** and **set*** functions to complement each new private member.

3 Expand the **CWarVehicle** class to include a customized **printdata** function. You will have to declare the original CVehicle::printdata as **virtual** so that it can be overridden in the derived class.

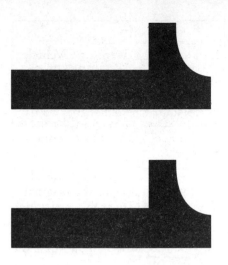

11 the I/O streams

In this chapter you will learn

- how to control formatting using cout and cin
- how to read and write files using iostreams

Aims of this chapter

The C++ I/O library has an object-oriented design that relies on many of the OOP concepts introduced previously, especially inheritance and operator overloads. This brief chapter explains how to control formatting options for **cout** and **cin** and also demonstrates string and file handling using I/O streams.

11.1 The new C++ I/O library

The I/O streams mechanism is a direct replacement for the C Standard Library functions defined in **stdio.h**. Although the version 1.x C++ language specifications never got them quite right, version 2.0 of C++ provided a flexible, functional set of streams that have been the standard ever since. It is worth noting, however, that as more and more software is written for use within a graphical environment such as Windows, the ability to perform basic console I/O is becoming less and less important.

In fact, the new library is simply a clever set of classes that organize input and output into streams. Streams can be thought of like drainpipes – once connected, anything can be thrown down them or sucked back out without worrying what the other end is connected to, or what type of data is being transferred. This is made possible through clever coding of the new library's classes (see also the heirarchy chart at the end of the chapter).

11.2 Console input/output

The main file **iostream.h** includes class definitions for the two main base classes: **ios**, and **streambuf**. The **ios** class holds basic input and output members, while the **streambuf** class manages the data buffer used by **ios**. Each instance of **ios** has a private member **bp**, which always points to an instance of **streambuf** or one of its derivatives. Standard input (previously handled by **scanf** in **stdio.h**) is actually handled by an instance of the class **istream**, which is derived from **ios**; standard output (previously **printf**) is now handled by an instance of **ostream**, also derived from ios.

A secondary class **iostream** is also defined in **iostream.h** – it is derived from both **istream** and **ostream**, and allows both input and output through the same object. Just as the C library defined **stdin**, **stdout**, and **stderr**, **iostream.h** automatically creates an instance of istream called **cin**, and instances of ostream called **cout** and **cerr**, which correspond to the same thing.

The various control flags used in the **printf/scanf** format specifiers translate to member functions of the **cout** and **cin** objects, which are called to set up the system before the I/O operation begins.

Printf specifier	Iostream equivalent
Flags	cout.flags(int flags)
Width	cout.width(int width)
Precision	cout.precision(int width)

```
/* streams.cpp (30/9/1999)
iostream demo */

#include <iostream.h>
int main()
{
    float num = 123.456f;
    cout << num << endl;
    cout.precision(2);    // set max precision to 2
    cout << num << endl;      // 'endl' adds a newline
    cout.width(10);             // set min width to 10
    cout << num << endl;
    return 0;
}
```

The output shows the result of the precision and width changes.

```
123.456001
123.46
123.46
```

11.3 String and file handling

Instead of **sprintf** and **sscanf**, you can include the file **strstream.h** (which is **strstrea.h** on DOS filing systems), which defines new string-handling classes from those in iostream.h –

strstreambase from ios, **istrstream** from istream and strstreambase, **ostrstream** from ostream and strstreambase, **strstream** from strstreambase and iostream, and **strstreambuf** from streambuf.

The syntax for using these classes is almost identical because so much of the code is inherited:

```
/* streams2.cpp (30/9/1999)
strstream demo */

#include <iostream.h>
#include <strstrea.h>

int main()
{
    float pi = 3.14159f;
    char text[40];
    strstream str1;        // create a new strstream object

    str1.precision(4);     // set input precision to 4
    str1 << pi;            // do: sprintf([string], "%.3f", pi);

    str1 >> text;         // copy the string to the text[] array
    cout << text;
    return 0;
}
```

Similarly, the file **fstream.h** includes definitions for stream classes that handle files. The operators << and >> replace **fprintf** and **fscanf**, and the other file functions in **stdio.h** – **fopen**, **fread**, **fwrite** and **fclose** – are all handled as part of the construction and destruction routines in the new classes.

```
/* streams3.cpp (30/9/1999)
using fstream.h */

#include <iostream.h>
#include <fstream.h>

int main()
{
    float num = 123.456f;
    fstream file1("demo.txt", ios::out);
    // ios::out is a predefined value
```

```
        file1 << num << endl;
        file1.precision(2);    // set max precision to 2
        file1 << num << endl;
        file1.width(10);       // set min width to 10
        file1 << num << endl;

        file1 << flush;        // 'flush' dumps stream to disk
        return file1.fail();   // return the success / failure code
    }
```

These examples are meant only to give an idea of the basic operation of the I/O streams, and the principles on which the work – covering every last detail is unnecessary. If you decide to use them, it is always worth consulting the on-line help for your compiler, which will list all the constructors, data members and functions defined in each class. Most of all, you should investigate **ios** and **streambuf**, because most of the functionality is inherited from these two bases.

In my experience, most programmers stick with stdio.h simply because the same can be achieved with fewer calls. However, the I/O streams are often faster; if speed is what you need, you might consider switching to the new system.

11.4 Class heirarchy chart

The full ancestry of the **iostream**, **strstream** and **fstream** classes looks like this:

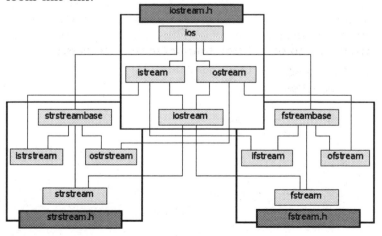

Each header file also defines a buffer class – **streambuf** in iostream.h, **strstreambuf** in strstream.h, and **filebuf** in fstream.h. **Streambuf** is the base class of the other two.

Summary

The I/O streams can take a lot of the work out of input and output, once they are set up. Although they are faster than the printf and scanf functions, the notation is less concise, and of course they only work in C++ (not C).

12

release-strength applications

In this chapter you will learn

- how to incorporate error-checking in your programs
- what a complete program looks like

Aims of this chapter

To write code that performs a certain operation is one thing; to build a program that is actually usable is quite another. This chapter lists a slightly larger sample program than before, to give you an idea of what real application code looks like. This is by no means industry standard stuff, but it incorporates enough error-checking and user-oriented design to produce a program that could be easily used by someone who had never come across it before.

12.1 The crypt program

The program is called **crypt** and is used to password-encrypt files specified on the command line. Exactly the same process is used to decrypt the files again. Files are encrypted/decrypted blindly; that is, crypt will run with whatever password it is given and will not attempt to determine whether or not that password is correct.

The encryption algorithm has been kept simple – so simple in fact, that it would be madness to use this program with any data that actually matters. Each byte of the file is just XOR-ed (see Appendix C) with one of the bytes of the password string until the end of the file is reached. This is a self-inversing process, which means that all you have to do to decrypt the file is to run it through the program again. What is made clear by this demonstration is that, to produce a release-strength application, the code to perform the actual operation is significantly shorter than the code one must write to make a final program.

12.2 Architecture

Although a program such as this is arguably too small to warrant the use of OOP, I have included a degree of object-based design as part of the demonstration. The code defines two classes: **CFile**, which encapsulates basic open/close and read/write functions, and **CCryptFile**, which incorporates the actual encryption code. This code is for **crypt.h**, a header file that makes all the necessary declarations for the project:

```
/* crypt.h - definitions for crypt.cpp */

#include <iostream.h>
#include <string.h>
#include <stdlib.h>
#include <dir.h>
#include <io.h>
#include <fcntl.h>

// compile-time options
#define VERSION 1
#define MAX_BUFFER 8192

// some definitions for our convenience
typedef unsigned char BYTE;
typedef unsigned short int BOOL;
#define TRUE 1
#define FALSE 0

class CFile
{
private:
    char name[256];
    int handle;
    BOOL CFile_EOF;

protected:
    CFile(char* new_name);
    ~CFile();

    char* getName() { return strdup(name); }
    BOOL IsEOF() { return CFile_EOF; }
    BOOL open(int mode);
    int read(BYTE* pTarget, int count);
    int write(BYTE* pSource, int count);
    int seek(int offset);
};

class CCryptFile : public CFile
{
protected:
    unsigned int uBuffsize;
```

```
        char password[8];
        BYTE* pBuffer;

    public:
        CCryptFile(char* new_password, char* new_name);
        ~CCryptFile();
        BOOL crypt();
};
```

CFile is the base for **CCryptFile** and provides basic file I/O functionality. The private data member **handle** stores the actual file handle, while the four functions **open**, **read**, **write** and **seek** do little more than call their Standard Library equivalents. The class has a constructor, which initializes the **name** member, and a destructor which automatically closes the file handle. The **getName** function returns a copy of **name**, and the **IsEOF** function returns the state of **CFile_EOF**, a Boolean variable that is set to 'true' when **read** reaches the end of file.

CCryptFile is derived from **CFile** and as a consequence, inherits all its protected members. The class also adds **pBuffer**, which points to a temporary buffer of size **uBuffsize**, and **password**, which stores the password string to be used for the encryption. The class adds a member function **crypt**, which does all the work, and has a constructor and a destructor to take care of initialization and memory allocation.

Notice that **CCryptFile**'s constructor is *public*; **CFile**'s constructor is *protected*. This means that although the main program can create as many instances of **CCryptFile** as memory space permits, it does not have sufficient access privileges to create instances of the base class **CFile**. **CCryptFile** instances are still initialized correctly because as a child of **CFile**, the **CCryptFile** constructor has access to the protected constructor of its parent. This arrangement prevents the inadvertent use of a class that is only meant as a base.

12.3 Implementation

With the class structure in place, it's time to look at the supporting code. The next listing is **cryptobj.cpp**, which contains the implementation of CFile and CCryptFile:

```
/* cryptobj.cpp - implementation of CFile and CCryptFile
 objects */

#include "crypt.h"

CFile::CFile(char* new_name)
{
    strcpy(name, new_name);
    handle = 0;
}

CFile::~CFile()
{
    if (handle) close(handle);
}

BOOL CFile::open(int mode)
{
    if (!handle) {
        handle = ::open(name, O_RDWR, mode);
    }
    return (BOOL)handle;
}

int CFile::read(BYTE* pTarget, int count)
{
    lseek(handle, 0, SEEK_CUR);
    int size = ::read(handle, pTarget, count);
    if (size != count) CFile_EOF = TRUE;
    return size;
}

int CFile::write(BYTE* pSource, int count)
{
    lseek(handle, 0, SEEK_CUR);
    return ::write(handle, pSource, count);
}

int CFile::seek(int offset)
{
    return lseek(handle, offset, SEEK_SET);
}
```

```
// =============================================

CCryptFile::CCryptFile(char* new_password, char*
new_name) : CFile(new_name)
{
    // copy the password string across
    strcpy(password, new_password);

    // try allocating 'uAttempt' bytes
    pBuffer = new BYTE[MAX_BUFFER];

    // if it didn't work, quit the program
    if (!pBuffer)
    {
        uBuffsize = MAX_BUFFER;
        cout << "Out of Memory";
        exit(-2);
    }
}

CCryptFile::~CCryptFile()
{
    if (pBuffer) delete[] pBuffer;
}

BOOL CCryptFile::crypt()
{
    int uRead = 0, uIndex = 0;
    int nChars = strlen(password);
    // open file, binary mode, read/write is automatic
    if (!open(O_BINARY))
    {
        cout << "Can't open!";
        return FALSE;
    }
    cout << getName() << "...";
    do
    {
        // read a block into the buffer
        uRead = read(pBuffer, uBuffsize);

        // XOR each buffer byte with a password byte
        for (int i = 0; i < uRead; i++)
```

```
    {
        pBuffer[i] ^= password[i%nChars];
    }

    // seek backwards and write that chunk
    seek(uIndex);
    write(pBuffer, uRead);
    uIndex += uRead;
}
while (!IsEOF());

cout << "OK.\n";
return TRUE;
}
```

The **CFile** member functions are all short, because they mirror the functionality provided by the Standard Library functions declared in the **io.h** header file. The **read** and **write** functions include a preliminary call to **lseek** to reset the file system, which is necessary when switching between read and write modes. Notice the use of the scope resolution operator, to help differentiate between the global **write** declared in **io.h**, and the protected **write** declared in the **CFile** definition:

```
int CFile::write(BYTE* pSource, int count)
{
    lseek(handle, 0, SEEK_CUR);
    return ::write(handle, pSource, count);
}
```

Without the :: operator, the name **write** would refer to the class member function **CFile::write**, and not to the external **write** function that we are trying to call.

The **CCryptFile::crypt** function does the main work of the program – here it is in 'pseudo code' to help you understand the structure:

```
if open() fails
{
    output error message;
    quit;
}
do
{
```

```
    read block from file into buffer;
    encrypt the buffer;
    seek file back to start of that block;
    write encrypted buffer back into the file;
}
until reached_end_of_file()
```

The first section calls the **open** function inherited from **CFile**; if this succeeds, the function enters a **do...while** loop to process the file. The first step is to read a block of data into the buffer previously allocated by the **CCryptFile** constructor, and encrypt it. This process involves a short **for** loop that iterates through each buffer byte in turn:

```
for (int i = 0; i < uRead; i++)
{
    pBuffer[i] ^= password[i%nChars];
}
```

The current buffer byte is XOR-ed with one of the characters from the password using the ^ operator. Notice how the index into the password string is given as **i%nChars** – this convenient use of the modulus operator ensures that once the value of i surpasses the total number of password characters, the next byte is XOR-ed with the first, and so on. For example, if the password was five characters long, the expression **i%nChars** would be counting 0, 1, 2, 3, 4, 0, 1, 2, 3, 4, 0, 1, 2... as i went from 0 to 12.

Once the buffer is encrypted, the next step is to write it back to the file. Following the last read operation, the file position will be at the end of that block, so we must move backwards with a call to the **seek** function. The variable **uIndex** maintains the current position across the read/encrypt operation, so we call **seek(uIndex);** to move back to the beginning. Once this is done, all that remains is to write the new block back over the old one using a call to **write**. This leaves the file position at the end of the block, ready for a new call to read on the next repetition of the loop.

This process continues until the member function **CFile::IsEOF** returns 'true', which is an indication that the end of the file has been reached. There is no need to close the file here; that is taken care of by the CFile destructor.

12.4 Operation

With a capable set of classes to perform the main work, the program stub has relatively little to do. The next listing contains a sample main function which parses the command line arguments and creates CCryptFile objects as necessary to deal with each target file:

```cpp
/* crypt.cpp (30/9/1999)
Crude File Encryption / Decryption */

#include "crypt.h"

// work through command line; create CCryptFile instances
as necessary
int main(int argc, char* argv[])
{
    CCryptFile* cf;
    ffblk findblock;
    char password[8];

    // anything to do?
    if (argc < 2)
    {
        cout << "\nCrypt Version " << VERSION << "\n\n";
        cout << "Usage: CRYPT [filenames]\n\n";
        return -1;
    }

    // ask for a password
    cout << "Enter Password: ";
    cin >> password;
    if (strlen(password) < 4)
    {
        cout << "\nError - password must be at least 4 chars long.";
        return -2;
    }

    // work through each file
    for(int i = 0; i < (argc-1); i++)
    {
        // clear ffblck structure and call findfirst()
        memset(&findblock, 0, sizeof(findblock));
        if (findfirst(argv[i+1], &findblock, 0))
        {
```

```
                cout << "Not Found: " << argv[i+1] << "\n";
                continue;
            }

            // finish working through this block
            do
            {
                // process this file
                cf = new CCryptFile(password, findblock.ff_name);
                if (!cf->crypt()) {
                    cout << "General Failure!";
                    return -2;
                }
                delete cf;

            // get the next file
            } while(!findnext(&findblock));
        }
        return 0;
    }
```

The first step is to check **argc**, the argument count. Since the
program name itself always counts as the first argument, we're
looking for at least two arguments if there's to be any actual
operation. Failing that, the program prints a short help message and exits with code –1.

Having prompted the user for a password, the function enters
a **for** loop to process each remaining command-line argument.
In order to deal with the possibility of wildcards – filenames
that include * or ? characters – we call the **findfirst** function
with the address of a **ffblk** structure to initialize the search. If
findfirst returns non-zero, no files matching the command-
line argument were found, so we print a warning and the 'continue' onto the next one.

If **findfirst** succeeds, we know that the operating system found
at least one file matching the specification, so the program
enters a second loop to work through as many files as are supplied by the **findnext** function.

The procedure for encrypting a file is trivial, thanks to the
design of the CCryptFile class. First, a new instance of
CCryptFile is allocated using the new operator. Assuming the

operation succeeds, a pointer to the new object is stored in the variable **cf**, which we then use to make the call to the **crypt** function belonging to the object. Finally, we de-allocate the CCryptFile object using the **delete** operator on **cf**, and re-start the loop with a new file.

Summary

Even in this short program, techniques including nested loops, dynamic memory allocation, blocked I/O and of course, OOP all play a valuable part. Although there is still a great deal of scope for improvement, the basic structure already demonstrated should provide a good foundation for expansion. Thanks to the object-oriented layout, progress could now be made without incurring great costs in organization and maintainability – this advantage far outweighs the initial hassle of setting up a class-based program structure.

Above all, this chapter demonstrates the significant difference between writing the code to perform a certain operation, and writing the complete program. While it may seem frustrating at first that the supporting framework occupies so much of the overall program code, the fact is that today's software spends as much time drawing pretty icons as it does performing the real work. Fortunately, you don't have to be a veteran programmer to be able to write user-interface code with your eyes closed – it's the graphic design that takes know-how, and if you ever go professional, that won't be your responsibility!

The final exercise

Dream up an incredible program, and write it. Researching and overcoming practical problems in the course of a project like this will eventually teach you far more than any book ever could. Remember, though, that there's always another way of doing things; usually, a far better one. Just don't give up!

appendices

A Taking it further

If you're just starting to get into programming, the good news is that everything gets easier from now on. Your C++ skills will provide an excellent foundation when moving to new languages or systems, and the more you write code, the quicker the learning process becomes.

The Internet is a great place to start developing your knowledge of the C++ language. Don't forget you can download most of the code used in this book, along with sample solutions to the exercises, at

http://tyc.oxtale.com/

The following newsgroups are highly recommended, but do check the relevant FAQ document and spend some time reading previous threads before posting to them:

alt.comp.lang.learn.c-c++ (for both beginners and experts)

comp.lang.c++ (more advanced discussion)

A good thick reference manual will help you to develop your skills further, particularly in specialist areas such as algorithm design and engineering research. Books in this field are expensive and the subject matter can be particularly dry, so do shop around and find a title that suits you. Don't forget, though, that most modern compiler packages have a wealth of on-line documentation included which may be sufficient for your project.

Windows and MacOS

Software that runs from the command line is extremely rare these days, and you'll soon want to write programs that make full use of the graphical user interface (GUI) of your target platform, be it Windows or MacOS. The old-fashioned approach to Windows programming is to link to the Windows API library and painstakingly build up windows, dialogs, buttons and controls using numerous function calls to CreateWindow() and its counterparts. Fortunately, the new breed of visual compiler tools can generate the interface code automatically while you concentrate on the core functionality of your program. Microsoft Visual C++ and Borland C++ Builder both include an extensive selection of project wizards and API wrappers to help you get started with a basic application framework.

Books on Windows programming tend to focus on a specific compiler package, and recognizing the fact that most readers already know basic C++, often concentrate more on how to use the compiler software than on actually writing code. Again, don't forget that the latest compiler packages include up to a gigabyte of online documentation and examples, so you may not need a printed copy of the same information.

Web applications

A background in C++ is particularly useful when getting started with web-based applications such as search engines and shopping carts. Although it is quite rare to use C++ for server-side programs, your skills are easily transferable to scripting languages such as Perl or PHP, both of which are supported across a wide variety of server platforms. A more advanced approach is to write compiled server modules ("plug-ins") in C, or to develop servlets for use on a Java-enabled web server such as Apache-Tomcat. The PHP home page at http://www.php.net/ is a good starting point for information on the hundreds of possibilities that await you.

If you want to publish your work you'll need to find a web host that supports your scripting language of choice, but for development purposes you should install a web server onto your local machine, so that you can edit and test your code without having to upload to a remote location.

It is often an advantage to have a near duplicate of the system that your final project will run on, and for this reason many developers switch to running Apache on Linux while developing web-based software. All the tools you need are open-source and available free of license fee from distributors including Red Hat, Debian and SuSE.

Games

Finally, and if you really relish a challenge, there is the question of games. I must confess that it was games programming that originally drew me into learning to write code, but it is still something of a black art in that a relatively small amount of literature exists, and that most of the hottest techniques are closely guarded secrets of the software houses. The situation has improved somewhat with the release of Microsoft's DirectX API, which provides a consistent interface to the 3D graphics, multi-channel sound, control input and networking hardware available on a Windows PC. To create a market-leading game is probably an impossible task for one person, but building a simple and original demo could be your ticket to a lucrative career in the games industry.

Using the shareware system

As your skill and experience grow, you will soon be able to write genuinely useful code, but the realistic size of a project for a single amateur programmer is often simply not big or complex enough to match the mammoth applications that consumers have come to expect from commercial vendors. Fortunately, there is still a channel through which you can sell your work to the world: shareware distribution.

The concept behind shareware software is that it is freely available to anyone, via distribution houses, BBS or the Internet, for an evaluation period. After that period, which usually lasts about 30 days, the user is obliged either to remove the software from their machine or to pay a fee to the author for registration. Shareware with no registration fee is often known as freeware, a policy usually reserved for tiny or novelty programs, such as screen savers. Unless the software is specifically donated to the public domain however, the author still retains the rights to the code, so no modification, reverse engineering or unaccredited redistribution is permissible.

The idea sounds perfect and indeed, it does provide an accessible way for authors to publish software – the Net holds libraries for hundreds of different platforms and operating systems. The prospect of releasing your creation to the world, and earning registration fees in the process, seems especially tantalizing. Before you plunge straight in though, it helps to be realistic about the number of registrations you are likely to receive – successful shareware authors estimate that at best, about 5% of people who use their software actually register it.

Despite the pitfalls, shareware authoring can still be very rewarding – morally if not financially. Perhaps the best part of all is receiving genuinely enthusiastic comments from people who could be anywhere in the world, thanks to the Internet's far reach. To maximize your chances of success, keep the following points in mind.

- You should document or automate the installation progress and make life as easy as possible for the end user. Try to make the program's interface intuitive and consistent.

- It is a good idea to declare copyright, and clearly state the limits of your liability for the program's use.

- Try to keep something back for the registered version – people are more likely to pay for things that they haven't already got than for those they have.

- Make the name of the registered user prominent to discourage casual distribution of a registered copy to friends and colleagues.

- If you use a registration key code system, be aware that crackers can defeat all but the most sophisticated dual-key military-spec encryption systems. You could try making regular version updates with different registration systems; this will slow but will not stop the crackers' progress.

- It is worth doing a little research before you finalize the registration fee for your software. Anything significantly more than the competition's will reduce the number of registrations, but ask too little and even the more honest people will think it hardly worth the effort.

Remember: shareware is a nice way to have fun with your programming skills, but don't, whatever you do, give up the day job!

The history of C++

I have already mentioned that C++ has a lot in common with plain C. Technically, C++ is a *superset* of C. It has all the features and syntax of C, plus new object-oriented capability and streamed I/O. This is actually reflected in the name, which when interpreted as a piece of code means 'one more than – or one better than – C'.

The original C language was designed, developed and implemented in 1972 by Dennis Ritchie and his team at Bell Telephone Laboratories, Inc. (now the AT&T labs), because the existing languages of the day were not really suited to their main task – writing the UNIX operating system. In the same year, the language was outlined in the book *The C Programming Language*, written by Brian Kernighan and Dennis Ritchie – if you can get hold of a copy, it's still an excellent source text. In fact, C was a development of two earlier languages that were also developed at Bell labs, 'BCPL' and 'B'.

Because it was designed specifically to write an operating system, C is well-suited to system-level program development, and is often called a system programming language. By combining the features of a high-level language with the ability to make low-level operating system calls, C bridged the gap between assembly language and high-level programming. As more people adopted it, the C language began to develop company- and institution-based dialects, due to the relatively loose definition of the C syntax set out by Kernighan and Ritchie. The problem grew rapidly worse, and threatened to destroy the language, until in 1983 the ANSI established a committee to negotiate and agree an industry standard for the language. Five years later, Kernighan and Ritchie published a second edition of their book, which included the standardized version, *ANSI C*.

By the early 1990s, C++ compilers had started to appear. The new specification went through several revisions, but by the time version 2.0 was released, C++ provided stronger type-checking, a new set of I/O libraries, and keywords for implementing object-oriented programming. Although the OOP capability made the language even more powerful, some argue that the C++ implementation of it is little more than C syntax with a few special keywords bolted on. To some extent, this is true – indeed, C++ is not really a truly object-oriented language, but a traditional language with new OOP extensions. If this bothers you and you are keen on the object-based model, you might like to take a look at Java, a much newer language which is object-oriented from the ground up.

For me, the idioms and inconsistencies of C++ are what gives it its strength. Like a spoken language, the oddities have developed because it is easier that way. C++ and its ancestor have been around for almost half the entire life of the electronic computer, during which time evolution has created a language so practical, so powerful, and so widespread that it is *barely* an exaggeration to say that nearly all serious software – and plenty that is not so serious – is written in it.

B Hexadecimal

I once heard that hexadecimal was invented purely to mystify non-programmers; the apparently meaningless combination of numbers and letters does instil a certain irrational fear in many. In fact, counting in base 16 (hexadecimal) is really very easy.

As humans, base ten (or *decimal*) is the logical system to use. Each digit in a number can represent one of ten values, and a number that is n digits long can have a value between 0 and 10^n. There are good evolutionary reasons for starting this way – mainly that normal humans have ten fingers. In a similar way, computers use base two (or *binary*) because they have memory that works by combining millions of two-state circuits. Why, then, is hexadecimal used at all? The reason is that converting numbers back and forth between binary and decimal is not easy to do. To achieve it, you must multiply the value of each digit by the appropriate power of two, and sum up the totals – a time-consuming task even for the mentally agile.

The advantage of using hex is that conversions to and from binary are relatively easy. Base 16 was chosen precisely because each digit represents exactly the same range as four binary digits. Thus, any conversion can be simplified greatly by dividing it into small parts. Since base 16 requires sixteen different digits, letters are used for the extra size that goes beyond our conventional, base ten digits. Counting in hex goes like this:

0, 1, 2, 3, 4, 5, 6, 7, 8, 9, A, B, C, D, E, F,
10, 11, 12, 13, 14, 15, 16, 17, 18, 19, 1A, 1B...

The most important thing to remember here is that 10 does *not* come after 9 when you are counting in hex! Small errors like this can lead to serious bugs in your code. Consider the binary number 0110101011101111. Can you look at it and give the decimal version? Probably not. With a little practice however, you will soon be able to work out the hexadecimal version:

The binary number is divided into groups of four bits:

0 1 1 0   1 0 1 0   1 1 1 0   1 1 1 1

Each 'nibble' is converted into a hex digit:

6   A   E   F

The final result is simply all the digits together:

6AEF

And, in case you are feeling too lazy to work out the hex representations of these nibbles, here is a handy table. There are only sixteen in total, so you will probably end up learning them off by heart without meaning to.

Decimal	Hex	Binary
0	0	0 0 0 0
1	1	0 0 0 1
2	2	0 0 1 0
3	3	0 0 1 1
4	4	0 1 0 0
5	5	0 1 0 1
6	6	0 1 1 0
7	7	0 1 1 1
8	8	1 0 0 0
9	9	1 0 0 1
10	A	1 0 1 0
11	B	1 0 1 1
12	C	1 1 0 0
13	D	1 1 0 1
14	E	1 1 1 0
15	F	1 1 1 1

In C++, hexadecimal constants are preceded by '0x' to differentiate them from decimals. You will find them most useful when working with individual bits and *bitmasks*. Suppose, for example, that you wanted to construct a bitmask that saved only the leftmost bit in an eight-bit value. The binary number would be 1000 0000 – and an easy conversion tells you that the hexadecimal is 80. The code to perform the operation would then be:

```
// test to see if the high bit of 'flags' is set
```

```
if (flags & 0x80)
{
    ...
}
```

The & operator you see here is the *bitwise combination operator*, not to be confused with &&, which is the *logical combination operator*. The bitwise version does the same comparison, but it works through each bit of its operands in turn. Thus, the only way for the expression (**flags** & **0x80**) to evaluate 'true' is if the leftmost bit of **flags**, AND the leftmost bit of **0x80** is set, which it is. The value **0x80** is called a bitmask because wherever one of its bit is zero, the effect is to mask off the corresponding bit in the other operand:

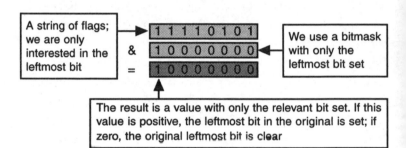

The four bitwise operators are explained further in Appendix C. They are:

&   AND

| OR

^   XOR (Exclusive Or)

~   NOT (1's Complement)

Hex values become more and more important as your understanding goes to a lower and lower level of computer hardware. However, complete comprehension is by no means a requirement of writing excellent software.

C Reference tables

This appendix contains a number of tables that you should find useful. Similar information can be found in your compiler's manual or on-line reference system.

Reserved words

The following keywords are reserved for use by the compiler, and cannot be used as variable or function names. Although some modern compilers specify still others, the standard C++ set looks like this:

asm	auto	break	case	char
class	const	continue	default	delete
do	double	else	enum	extern
float	for	friend	goto	if
inline	int	interrupt	long	main
naked	new	operator	private	protected
public	register	return	short	signed
sizeof	static	struct	switch	template
this	typedef	union	unsigned	virtual
void	volatile	while		

In case you're wondering, **auto** is simply the default modifier if neither **extern** nor **static** is used, and is rarely used explicitly. Similarly, **short** is just the opposite of **long** and **signed** the opposite of **unsigned**. Since they are the default on most systems, adding them has no effect.

You can use **volatile** as an extra type modifier if the memory location you wish to access may be altered simultaneously by some other program. If this is the case, declaring the variable as volatile disables any compiler optimizations, ensures that the value is re-read from memory each time the code uses it, and guarantees that it is written immediately back again after modification. Without the **volatile** modifier, the compiler will attempt to speed up your code by temporarily storing values in the CPU registers – you can give variables priority in this process using the **register** modifier. However, the compiler knows best and will only satisfy your request if it fits neatly into the optimization plan.

Character codes

The most common non-numeric use for bytes is the storage of characters. The following charts lists the codes for each character, according to the ASCII standard, for the range 0 to 127 or 0 to 7F hexadecimal. The characters above 128 vary according to the character set.

Standard ASCII chart (characters 0 to 127)
0 to 31 are non-printing control characters.

Decimal	Hex	Character	Decimal	Hex	Character
000	00	(nul)	031	1F	(us)
001	01	(soh)	032	20	sp
002	02	(stx)	033	21	!
003	03	(etx)	034	22	"
004	04	(eot)	035	23	#
005	05	(enq)	036	24	$
006	06	(ack)	037	25	%
007	07	(bel)	038	26	&
008	08	(bs)	039	27	'
009	09	(tab)	040	28	(
010	0A	(lf)	041	29	)
011	0B	(vt)	042	2A	*
012	0C	(np)	043	2B	+
013	0D	(cr)	044	2C	,
014	0E	(s0)	045	2D	-
015	0F	(si)	046	2E	.
016	10	(dle)	047	2F	/
017	11	(dc1)	048	30	0
018	12	(dc2)	049	31	1
019	13	(dc3)	050	32	2
020	14	(dc4)	051	33	3
021	15	(nal)	052	34	4
022	16	(syn)	053	35	5
023	17	(etb)	054	36	6
024	18	(can)	055	37	7
025	19	(em)	056	38	8
026	1A	(eof)	057	39	9
027	1B	(esc)	058	3A	:
028	1C	(fs)	059	3B	;
029	1D	(gs)	060	3C	<
030	1E	(rs)	061	3D	=

Decimal	Hex	Character	Decimal	Hex	Character
062	3E	>	095	5F	_
063	3F	?	096	60	`
064	40	@	097	61	a
065	41	A	098	62	b
066	42	B	099	63	c
067	43	C	100	64	d
068	44	D	101	65	e
069	45	E	102	66	f
070	46	F	103	67	g
071	47	G	104	68	h
072	48	H	105	69	i
073	49	I	106	6A	j
074	4A	J	107	6B	k
075	4B	K	108	6C	l
076	4C	L	109	6D	m
077	4D	M	110	6E	n
078	4E	N	111	6F	o
079	4F	O	112	70	p
080	50	P	113	71	q
081	51	Q	114	72	r
082	52	R	115	73	s
083	53	S	116	74	t
084	54	T	117	75	u
085	55	U	118	76	v
086	56	V	119	77	w
087	57	W	120	78	x
088	58	X	121	79	y
089	59	Y	122	7A	z
090	5A	Z	123	7B	{
091	5B	[	124	7C	|
092	5C	\	125	7D	}
093	5D	]	126	7E	~
094	5E	^	127	7F	delete

These codes are especially useful when you need to print special characters. Although you already have the character escape sequences at your disposal, such as \t for tab, any character can be accessed if you know its hexadecimal code. How? The character's code is simply preceded by the special escape sequence \x. For example:

```
// Initialize a char array
char test[] = "\x68\x65\x6c\x6c\x6f"

// The content of test[] is now:
// "hello"
```

Thanks to the clever arrangement of the ASCII codes, a few quick tricks are possible that can come in handy for manipulating strings. Don't forget, though, that the Standard Library holds a whole host of functions for string conversion.

Letters to numbers

You will see from the chart that the ASCII code 048 corresponds to the digit zero, 049 for one, and so on up to 057 for nine. This feature means that any single character can be converted to a numeric value simply by subtracting 48 from the character code, and vice versa. Remember that this trick only works with single-digit numbers!

Alphabet letters

The second point of interest is in the alphabet letters. It may seem odd that the letter 'a' does not follow straight on from the letter 'Z' – the reason for delaying the lower case slightly is so that the upper and lower case letters differ only in the sixth bit of the eight-bit code number. For example:

Letter	Decimal	Hexadecimal	Binary
R	82	0x52	0 1 0 1 0 0 1 0
r	114	0x72	0 1 1 1 0 0 1 0

To force a character to upper case, then, takes only the following code:

```
// DF is hexadecimal for 1101 1111 binary
Key &= 0xDF;
```

This is yet another example of using a bitmask to set or clear individual bits in a number. For more information, see Appendix B.

Logical operators

The AND, OR, XOR and NOT functions were mentioned briefly in the previous appendix for use with bitmasks. These logical commands go right back to basic digital electronics, and are frequently used in the construction of trivial and advanced circuits alike. This section presents their behaviour in full and explains their common uses in C++.

It is important to understand that although AND, OR, XOR and NOT are technically functions in the wider sense, taking input and returning output, C++ actually implements them as operators. This means that rather than making a function call every time you wanted to use, for example, the AND function, like this...

```
// calling an imaginary "and" function
// with arguments A and B. Wrong!
result = and(A, B);
```

...the programmer can use this much simpler form.

```
result = A & B;
```

I shall begin with the NOT function as it is the simplest and probably the most widely used. NOT takes a single argument, and returns the opposite of that argument. C++ provides two versions: bitwise NOT, represented by the operator ~, and logical NOT, represented by the operator !. The difference is that the bitwise version works through every bit of the operand in turn, inverting each one from one to zero or zero to one. The logical version works on the value of its operand as a whole, interpreting any non-zero operand as 'true', and zero as 'false'. The opposite is then returned.

Consider, for example, the binary value 01010111. The bitwise NOT operator would return a value made up of the inverse of the original – in this case, 10101000. The logical operator would interpret the value as 'true', because it is non-zero, and would therefore return zero ('false').

The next function, AND, gives a result of one ('true') only when both operands, called A and B in the table below, are also 1. It has two representations in C++. The bitwise operator & performs comparisons that work bit by bit through the pair of operands, and is very often used to apply bitmasks. The logical operator && works on the total values of its two operands, and is most often used to compare multiple events in a conditional statement such as if or while. When comparing values logically, zero is interpreted as 'false', and any other value – positive or negative – as 'true'. This table lists all the possible outcomes:

A	B	OUT
0	0	0
0	1	0
1	0	0
1	1	1

The obvious companion to AND is the OR function. As you might expect, it gives a result of 1 ('true') when either of the inputs is also 1. The bitwise version | is used to force certain bits to 'set' in a long string of flags without affecting the others.

How is this done? The bitmask must consist of clear bits where you do not want to make any changes, and set bits where you want to enable the flags in the real string. Thus, clear bits in the original remain clear unless you have set the appropriate bit in the bitmask. Set bits in the original remain set regardless of the corresponding value in the bitmask.

The logical version || is most often used in conditional statements when any or all of a collection of events must trigger the conditional branch of the code. For example:

```
if (A || B || C)
{
    // we get to here if either A, B, or C are non-zero.
    ...
}
```

Here is the complete truth table for OR:

A	B	OUT
0	0	0
0	1	1
1	0	1
1	1	1

Finally, the XOR or 'exclusive or' function. Like OR, XOR returns 1 ('true') if either of the inputs is also 1. Unlike OR however, XOR does *not* return 1 if both inputs have a value of 1. C++ only provides a bitwise version of the XOR function, represented by the operator ^. The bitwise XOR operator, like its cousins, is useful when working with single bits in a long string of flags.

Suppose, for example, that you want to flip a certain bit in an eight-bit value. The bitmask to accomplish this task must consist of a set bit where you want to change the original, and clear bits where you want to leave the original alone.

1 If the bit in the original that you want to change is already set, XOR-ing it with the mask will clear it, because 1 ^ 1 = 0.

2 If the bit in the original that you want to change is clear, it will end up set, because 0 ^ 1 = 1.

3 All the other bits, whether set or clear, will be unaffected because the corresponding bit in the bitmask is also clear. Thus, 0 ^ 0 = 0 (no change) and 1 ^ 0 = 1 (again, no change).

Here is the table in full:

A	B	OUT
0	0	0
0	1	1
1	0	1
1	1	0

Printf format specifiers

The format specifiers used in the format strings for the printf and scanf were introduced in Chapter 7. The syntax for a format specifier is:

%[flags][width][.precision][size][type]

flags	leading zeros, justification mode, etc.
width	minimum number of characters to fill
precision	maximum number of characters to fill
size	modifies the size of the 'type' field
type	required specification of data type

The full list of options for the three non-numeric fields is given below.

Flags Description

–	Left align the result within the given output width
+	Prefix the output with '+' for positives and '–' for negatives
0	Use 0s to pad output of floating point numbers to correct width
#	With types o, x and X – prefix output with '0', '0x' and '0X'
	With types e, E and f – force output to contain a decimal point
	With types g and G – force decimal point and do not remove trailing zeros.

Size	Combination	Result
l	with types d, i, o, x and X	long int
h	with types d, i, o, x and X	short int
l	with type u	long unsigned int
h	with type u	short unsigned int

Type	Typical use	Description
c	char	single character
C	wchar_t	single multi-byte character
d	int	signed decimal integer
i	int	signed decimal integer
o	unsigned int	unsigned octal integer
u	unsigned int	unsigned decimal integer
x	unsigned int	unsigned hexadecimal integer, using letters "abcdef"
X	unsigned int	unsigned hexadecimal integer, using letters "ABCDEF"
e	double	signed floating-point number in exponential form (±a.bbbe±ccc)
E	double	signed floating-point number in exponential form, with E instead of e
f	double	signed floating-point value of the form ±aaaa.bbbb
g	double	value printed in either e or f format, whichever is most compact
G	double	value printed in either E or f format, whichever is most compact
p	void*	hexadecimal segmented memory address in the form aaaa:bbbb
s	char*	null-terminated string
S	char*	null-terminated string of multibyte characters

index